The
LORD'S DAY

The
LORD'S DAY

Thomas Boston – Ettrick
James Fisher – Glasgow
John Kennedy – Dingwall

REFORMATION PRESS

2016

British Library Cataloguing in Publication Data

ISBN 978-1-872556-13-0

© Reformation Press 2016

Published by Reformation Press
11 Churchill Drive, Stornoway
Isle of Lewis, Scotland HS1 2NP

www.reformationpress.co.uk

First Kindle edition
ISBN 978-1-872556-18-5
June 2016

Printed by www.lulu.com

Remember the sabbath day, to keep it holy. Six days shalt thou labour, and do all thy work: But the seventh day is the sabbath of the LORD *thy God: in it thou shalt not do any work, thou, nor thy son, nor thy daughter, thy manservant, thy maidservant, nor thy cattle, nor thy stranger that is within thy gates: For in six days the* LORD *made heaven and earth, the sea, and all that in them is, and rested the seventh day: wherefore the* LORD *blessed the sabbath day, and hallowed it.*

Exodus 20:8-11

Contents

Foreword

God blessed the seventh day, and sanctified it: because that in it he had rested from all his work which God created and made.
Genesis 2:3

God blessed and sanctified the seventh day of the creation week. He established this holy day of rest – the Sabbath Day – and set it apart as the day on which Adam and Eve were to worship him. After the fall of man, the Sabbath remained an integral part of the religion of the patriarchs – there are numerous allusions to this in Genesis and Exodus, before the Ten Commandments were given at Sinai.

In the formal delivery of the Ten Commandments at Mount Sinai, the fourth commandment is expressed in terms which clearly indicate that the Sabbath was already known and observed. '*Remember* the sabbath day, to keep it holy' (Exodus 20:8). These words show that God was solemnly reaffirming the obligation to keep the day holy. After the resurrection of Christ, the day set apart for the worship of God became the first day of the week – the Lord's Day, the Christian Sabbath.

A succinct statement of the teaching of the Bible on the subject of the Sabbath Day is contained in Chapter 21 of the Westminster Confession of Faith:

> Section 7: As it is the law of nature that, in general, a due proportion of time be set apart for the worship of God; so in his Word, by a positive, moral, and perpetual commandment, binding to all men, in

9

all ages, he hath particularly appointed one day in seven for a Sabbath, to be kept holy unto him; which from the beginning of the world to the resurrection of Christ, was the last day of the week; and from the resurrection of Christ, was changed into the first day of the week, which in Scripture is called the Lord's Day, and is to be continued to the end of the world as the Christian Sabbath.

Section 8: This Sabbath is then kept holy unto the Lord, when men after a due preparing of their hearts, and ordering of their common affairs beforehand, do not only observe an holy rest all the day from their worldly employments and recreations; but also are taken up the whole time in the public and private exercises of his worship, and in the duties of necessity and mercy.[1]

This book contains material on the subject of the Lord's Day from men who had a clear grasp of the Scriptural basis for observing the Sabbath Day – Thomas Boston of Ettrick, James Fisher of Glasgow and John Kennedy of Dingwall. The subject matter has been lightly edited with some alterations to layout, grammar and vocabulary to bring it in line with twenty-first century usage.

Thomas Boston

Thomas Boston was born in 1676 in the town of Duns in the south-eastern corner of Scotland. His family were privileged to be under the teaching of Rev Henry Erskine, father of the renowned brothers Ebenezer and Ralph Erskine. Under this faithful ministry, Thomas Boston was spiritually awakened at the age of eleven. He was called to

---

1   These sections of the Confession of Faith are reproduced with Scripture proofs in the Appendix of the present publication.

the work of the ministry and in due course was ordained and began his ministry in the Scottish border parish of Simprin in 1699.

Boston's days in Simprin marked the beginning of labours which were to bear fruits far beyond the confines of this small and secluded parish. He fulfilled his pastoral duties faithfully and began a prayerful study of the Word of God which continued after he became Minister in the upland parish of Ettrick. From these remote parishes issued masterpieces of Christian literature. Some of these remain in print at the present day, such as *Human nature in its fourfold state*, *A soliloquy on the art of man-fishing*, and *A view of the covenant of grace*. Many of Boston's works are available online or as e-books. His instructive autobiography remains in print as *Memoirs of Thomas Boston*.

Thomas Boston wrote *A Body of Divinity* as 'an illustration of the doctrines of the Christian Religion'. The order in which he deals with these doctrines parallels the contents of the *Shorter Catechism* of the Westminster Assembly. The *Body of Divinity* is a masterly work, methodical in its approach to the doctrines of Christianity. It bears a clear testimony to the intellectual stature and piety of its author. He covers the subjects in a comprehensive manner, and always with a view to impressing upon his readers the practical aspects of the doctrines.

This book contains Boston's treatise on the fourth commandment, taken from the *Body of Divinity*. He deals with the subject in great detail and yet, throughout the discourse, he holds the reader's attention.

James Fisher

James Fisher (1697-1775) was born into the manse of the small Ayrshire village of Barr. He studied at Glasgow University and was ordained as Minister of Kinclaven in Perthshire in 1725. Two years later he married the daughter of Rev Ebenezer Erskine of Portmoak, Kinross-shire. On account of doctrinal laxity in the Church of Scotland, Fisher and Erskine seceded in 1733 and were among the founders of the Associate Presbytery, which later became the United Secession Church. Fisher subsequently became a minister in Glasgow in 1741.

Fisher is best known nowadays as the principal editor of a book commonly known as *Fisher's Catechism*, which explains the *Shorter Catechism* of the Westminster Assembly of Divines. Fisher edited this *Catechism* in collaboration with the well-known ministers Ralph and Ebenezer Erskine. The first part of the catechism appeared in 1753 and dealt with the first thirty-eight questions in the *Shorter Catechism*. Fisher survived the Erskine brothers and was responsible for bringing the second part of the work (dealing with the remainder of the *Shorter Catechism*) to publication in 1760. The book quickly became a popular work of instruction far beyond the original denomination.

John Kennedy

Dr John Kennedy of Dingwall was one of the greatest of the Evangelical Ministers in the Scottish Highlands in the second half of the nineteenth century. He was born in Killearnan, Ross-shire, in 1819. His father (also named John Kennedy) was the eminently saintly Minister of that parish. However the young John Kennedy was 'a stranger to grace and to God' when he entered the Divinity Hall of Aberdeen in 1840. The death of his father in 1841 led him to seek the salvation of his soul. After his father's funeral, John Kennedy returned to Aberdeen renewed by the grace of God. In the words of his biographer, 'His former indifference to Divine things had given place in his mind to deep seriousness, his self-sufficiency to self-abasement, the things of time to the things of eternity – old things had passed away, all things had become new.' From then on, he led a life of usefulness to the Cause of Christ. He was a faithful exponent of the Word of God and was diligent in all his labours.

Dr Kennedy is now largely remembered as a chronicler of religious life in the Scottish Highlands. His biography of Dr Macdonald of Ferintosh – *The Apostle of the North* – and *The Days of the Fathers in Ross-shire* remain available in printed and electronic formats. However, in his own day, he was outstandingly a preacher of the Gospel and selections of his sermons are currently in print, including *The Saviour* by *Reformation Press*. Kennedy was also a valiant defender of 'the truth as it is in Jesus' at a time when the Scriptures were under attack, not only from an unbelieving world but also from enemies within the visible church. Dr Kennedy was one of the servants of Christ who were raised up to defend the doctrines of the Bible in those days of rampant infidelity.

Dr Kennedy was well acquainted with Biblical teaching about the Christian Sabbath and he defended it with vigour. The lecture on the fourth commandment was delivered in Dingwall in 1883. In it, Dr Kennedy refers to a significant incident at Strome Ferry in Wester Ross which occurred three months previously. The railway company was involved in goods traffic on the Lord's Day. Despite representations from the Church, the desecration of the Lord's Day increased. Eventually, one Sabbath, about two hundred young men of the community took quiet possession of the pier, and told the railway officials that they would allow no work on the Lord's Day. Scuffles broke out when the Police attempted to intervene and ten of the protesters were imprisoned. Dr Kennedy did all he could for them, addressing public meetings held on their behalf and helping in many practical ways. Norman Campbell has written a review of this incident entitled *The Strome Ferry Case* in the *Scottish Reformation Society Historical Journal,* Vol. 3 (2013), pp. 299-130.[2]

Dr Kennedy's address touches on the issues raised by the Strome Ferry Case and the relation of the Christian community to desecration of the Lord's Day which is not checked by lawful civil authorities. His thought-provoking lecture deals with many other aspects of observance of the Christian Sabbath. John Kennedy's lecture complements the methodical examinations of the doctrines of the fourth commandment contained in Thomas Boston's treatise and James Fisher's catechism.

CX∞CX∞

Reformation Press originally published *The Lord's Day* as a booklet consisting of Boston's treatise and Kennedy's lecture. It was issued in 1991 in the context of major attacks on Sabbath observance in Scotland. The booklet proved very popular, not only in Scotland but also in other countries. Now nearly a quarter of a century later there are increasingly hostile attempts to abolish the remaining laws and statutes protecting the Lord's Day. In these days of doctrinal and practical laxity there is a great need to give sound biblical teaching on the Lord's Day. The new edition of *The Lord's Day* is supplemented by material from *Fisher's Catechism* and also contains the relevant sections of the *Westminster Confession of Faith.* The book reaffirms the Scriptural basis for Sabbath observance – it is because **God** has said, 'Remember the sabbath day, to keep it holy'.

THE PUBLISHER
Stornoway
June 2016

---

[2]   This article is available as a download from the website of the Scottish Reformation Society (www.scottishreformationsociety.org).

Part 1

Treatise on the fourth commandment

Thomas Boston, Ettrick

Introduction

This command relates to the time of worship, and is the last of the first table of the Ten Commandments, set to join both tables of the commandments together, the Sabbath being the bond of all religion. In the words we have the command and the reasons annexed to the command.

The command

It is delivered in two ways, positively and negatively.

The positive command

The command is delivered positively: 'Remember the sabbath day, to keep it holy.' The word 'Sabbath' signifies rest of cessation from labour.

There is a threefold rest or Sabbath spoken of in Scripture: temporal – the weekly Sabbath.; spiritual – which is an internal soul rest, in ceasing from sin;[3] and eternal – celebrated in heaven, where the saints rest from their labours.[4] It is the first of these, the weekly Sabbath, that is here meant. Observe here:

(a) Our duty with respect to the Sabbath. It is *'to keep it holy'*. God has made it holy, set it apart for holy exercises, and we must keep it holy, spending it in holy exercises.

---

3   Hebrews 4:3. For we which have believed do enter into rest, as he said, As I have sworn in my wrath, if they shall enter into my rest: although the works were finished from the foundation of the world.

4   Hebrews 4:9-11. There remaineth therefore a rest to the people of God. For he that is entered into his rest, he also hath ceased from his own works, as God did from his. Let us labour therefore to enter into that rest, lest any man fall after the same example of unbelief.

(b) The quantity of time to be observed as a Sabbath of rest – a day, a whole day of twenty-four hours; and the one day in seven. They must observe a seventh day after six days' labour, wherein all our work must be done and finished so as nothing of it may remain to be done on the Sabbath.

(c) A note of remembrance put upon it; which indicates that this precept should be diligently observed, special regard paid to it, and due honour put upon this sacred day.

The negative command

The command is delivered negatively. Here observe two things:

(a) What is forbidden here – the doing of any work that may hinder the sanctifying of this day.

(b) To whom the command is directed, and who must observe it – magistrates to whom belong the gates of the city, and masters of families to whom belong the gates of the house. They must observe it themselves and cause others to observe it.

The reasons annexed to this command

None of the commands is thus delivered, both positively and negatively, as this one is. And that indicates the following three matters:

(a) God is in a special manner concerned for the keeping of the Sabbath, it being that on which all religion depends. Accordingly, as it is observed or disregarded, so it readily goes with the other parts of religion.

(b) People are most ready to halve the service of this day, either to look on resting from labour as sufficient, or to look on the work of the day as over when the public work is over.

(c) There is less light of nature for this command than the rest: for though it is naturally moral that there should be a Sabbath, yet it is but positively moral that this should be one day in seven, depending entirely on the will of God.

In discoursing further from this subject, I shall show:

1. What is required in the fourth commandment
2. Which day of the seven God has appointed to be the weekly Sabbath
3. How the Sabbath is to be sanctified
4. What is forbidden in this command
5. The reasons annexed to the command
6. A practical application

Chapter 1

What is required in the fourth commandment?

I am to show what is required in the fourth commandment. This command, according to our Catechism, requires 'the keeping holy to God such set times as he hath appointed in his word; expressly one whole day in seven, to be a holy sabbath to himself'.

Here I shall show:

1. This command requires the keeping holy to God such set times as he has appointed in his word.
2. It requires one day in seven to be kept as a holy Sabbath to the Lord.
3. The day to be kept holy is one whole day.

God has appointed times which are to be kept holy

First, I am to show that this command requires the keeping holy to God such set times as he has appointed in his word.

The Jews under the Old Testament had several days, beside the weekly Sabbath, that by divine appointment were to be kept as holy days. And by virtue of this command they were to observe them, even as by virtue of the second commandment they were to observe the sacrifices and other parts of the Old Testament instituted worship. But these days are taken away under the Gospel by the coming of Christ.

But that which this commandment in the first place requires is the keeping holy of a Sabbath to God, whatever be the day God determines for it; whether the seventh in order from the creation, as under the Old Testament, or the first, as under the New. And so the command is

'Remember the sabbath day, to keep it holy'; not 'Remember the seventh day'. Thus the keeping of a sabbath is moral duty binding all persons in all places of the world. For it is moral duty and it is required by the natural law, that as God is to be worshipped – not only internally but externally, not only privately but publicly – so there must be some special time designed and set apart for this, without which it cannot be done. And so the very pagans had theirs sabbaths and holy days. This is the first thing signified here, namely that a sabbath is to be kept.

Another thing signified here is that it belongs to God to determine the Sabbath, or what day or days he will have to be kept holy. He does not say, 'Remember to keep holy *a* sabbath day' or '*a* day of rest', leaving it to men to decide what days shall be holy and what shall not; but 'Remember *the* sabbath day', supposing the day to be already determined by himself. So that we are bound to the set time appointed in his Word. And this condemns men's taking on themselves, whether as churches or states, to appoint holy days to be kept, which God has not appointed in his word.

Consider the four following matters:

(a) This command puts a peculiar honour on the Sabbath above all other days, 'Remember the sabbath day'. But when men make holy days of their own to be kept holy, the day appointed of God is spoiled of its peculiar honour, and there is no peculiar honour left to it.[5] Yea, in practice they go before it; for men's holy days, where they are regarded, are more regarded than God's day.

(b) This command says, 'Six days shalt thou labour'. Formalists say, 'There are many of these six days thou shalt not labour, for they are holy days.' If these words contain a command, who can countermand

---

5   Ezekiel 43:8. In their setting of their threshold by my thresholds, and their post by my posts, and the wall between me and them, they have even defiled my holy name by their abominations that they have committed.

it? If these words contain but a permission, who can take away that liberty which God has left us? As for fast days or thanksgiving days appointed on particular occasions, they are not holy days; the worship is not made to wait upon the days, as on Sabbaths and holy days, but the days are made to wait on the worship which God by his providence requires; and consequently there must be a time for performing these exercises.

(c) It belongs only to God to make a holy day, for who can sanctify a creature but the Creator, or who can sanctify time but the Lord of time? He only can give the blessing. Why should they then sanctify a day who cannot bless it? The Lord abhors holy days devised out of men's own hearts.[6]

(d) What reason is there to think, when God has taken away from the Church's neck a great many holy days appointed by himself, that he has left the Gospel Church to be burdened with as many – nay, and more – of men's invention, than he himself had appointed?

One day in seven must be kept as a holy Sabbath

This command requires one day in seven to be kept as a holy Sabbath unto the Lord: 'Six days shalt thou labour, and do all thy work: but the seventh day is the sabbath of the LORD thy God.' Thus the Lord determines the quantity of time that is to be his own, in a peculiar manner, that is, the seventh part of our time. After six days' working, a seventh is to be a Sabbath. This is moral, binding all persons in all ages, and not a ceremony abrogated by Christ.

(a) This command of appointing one day in seven for a Sabbath is one of the commands of that law, consisting of ten commands, which

---

6   1 Kings 12:33. So he offered upon the altar which he had made in Bethel the fifteenth day of the eighth month, even in the month which he had devised of his own heart; and ordained a feast unto the children of Israel: and he offered upon the altar, and burnt incense.

cannot be made out without this; it was written on tables of stone, to show the perpetuity of it; and of which Christ says (Matthew 5:17-19), 'Think not that I am come to destroy the law, or the prophets: I am not come to destroy, but to fulfil. For verily I say unto you, Till heaven and earth pass, one jot or one tittle shall in no wise pass from the law, till all be fulfilled. Whosoever therefore shall break one of these least commandments, and shall teach men so, he shall be called the least in the kingdom of heaven: but whosoever shall do and teach them, the same shall be called great in the kingdom of heaven.'

(b) It was appointed and given by God to Adam in his state of innocence, before there was any ceremony to be taken away by the coming of Christ.[7]

(c) All the reasons annexed to this command are moral, respecting all men, as well as the Jews to whom the ceremonial law was given. And we find strangers obliged to the observation of it, as well as the Jews; but they were not obliged to the observation of ceremonial laws.

(d) Jesus Christ speaks of it as a thing perpetually to endure, even after the Jewish Sabbath was over and gone.[8]

One whole day must be kept holy

The day to be kept holy is one whole day. Not a few hours, while the public worship lasts, but a whole day. There is an artificial day between sunrise and sunset.[9] And there is a natural day of twenty-four hours,[10] which is the day here meant. This day we begin in the morning immediately after midnight; and so does the Sabbath begin, and not in the evening, as is clear if you consider the following three matters:

---

7   Genesis 2:3. And God blessed the seventh day, and sanctified it: because that in it he had rested from all his work which God created and made.'

8   Matthew 24: 20. But pray ye that your flight be not in the winter, neither on the sabbath day.'

9   John 11:9. Are there not twelve hours in the day?

10 Genesis 1:5. And the evening and the morning were the first day.

(a) John 20:19: 'The same day at evening, being the first day of the week' – where you see that the evening following, not going before this first day of the week, is called the evening of the first day.

(b) Our Sabbath begins where the Jewish Sabbath ended; but the Jewish Sabbath did not end towards the evening, but towards the morning (Matthew 28:11): 'In the end of the sabbath, as it began to dawn toward the first day of the week', etc.

(c) Our Sabbath is held in memory of Christ's resurrection, and it is certain that Christ rose early in the morning of the first day of the week.

Let us therefore take the utmost care to give God the whole day, spending it in the manner he has appointed, and not look on all the time, apart from what is spent in public worship, as our own – which is too much the case in these degenerate times wherein we live.

Chapter 2

Which day of the seven has God appointed to be the weekly Sabbath?

I come now to show which day of the seven God has appointed to be the weekly Sabbath. According to our Catechism, 'From the beginning of the world to the resurrection of Christ, God appointed the seventh day of the week to be the weekly sabbath; and the first day of the week ever since, to continue to the end of the world, which is the Christian sabbath.'

We have heard that this command requires a Sabbath to be kept – that is, one whole day in seven. We are now to consider what day that is. The Scripture teaches us that there are two days which by divine appointment have had this honour – the seventh day, and the first day of the week.

Sabbath – the seventh day of the week

As to the seventh day, it is acknowledged by all that this was the Jewish Sabbath. And concerning it, consider the following four matters.

1. Who appointed the seventh day to be the Sabbath?
It was God himself that appointed the seventh day, which is the last day of the week (by us called Saturday) to be the Sabbath: 'The seventh day is the sabbath of the LORD thy God.' He that was the Lord of time made this designation of the time at first.

2. Wherefore did God at first appoint the seventh day?
The reason of this was that, as God rested that day from all his works of creation, men might, after his example, rest on that day from their own

works in order that they might remember his works and celebrate the praises of the Creator. 'For in six days the Lord made heaven and earth […] and rested the seventh day.' The work of creation was performed in the six days, and nothing was made in the seventh day, so that the first new day that man saw was a holy day, a Sabbath, so that he might know that the great end [purpose] of his creation was to serve the Lord.

3. How long did that appointment of the seventh day last?

It lasted to the resurrection of Christ. This was its last period, at which time it was to give place to a new institution, as will afterwards appear. The day of Christ's resurrection was the day of the finishing of the new creation, the restoration of a marred world.

4. When was the Sabbath of the seventh day appointed first?

Some who detract from the honour of the Sabbath contend that it was not appointed till the promulgating of the law on Mount Sinai, and that its first institution was in the wilderness. We hold that it was appointed from the beginning of the world. For proof of this, consider the following:

(a) Moses tells us plainly that God, immediately after perfection of the works of creation, blessed and hallowed the seventh day.[11] Now, how could it be blessed and hallowed but by an appointing of it to be the Sabbath, setting it apart from common works to the works of God's solemn worship? The words run on in a continued history, without the least shadow of anticipating, upwards of two thousand years, as some would have it.

(b) The Sabbath of the seventh day was observed before the promulgation of the law from Sinai, and is spoken of (Exodus 16) not as a

---

11   Genesis 2:2-3. And on the seventh day God ended his work which he had made; and he rested on the seventh day from all his work which he had made. And God blessed the seventh day, and sanctified it: because that in it he had rested from all his work which God created and made.

new institution but as an ancient institution. So preparation for the Sabbath is called for, before any mention of it is made, clearly signifying that it was known before.[12] See verse 23 where the Sabbath is given for a reason why they should prepare the double quantity of manna on the sixth day; which says that solemn day was not first instituted then.[13] And the breach of the Sabbath is exposed as the violation of a law formerly given.[14]

c) In the fourth commandment they are called to remember the Sabbath Day as a day that was not first appointed at that time, but had been appointed before, although it had gone out of use and had been much forgotten when they were in Egypt. Besides, the reason of this command – God's resting the seventh day and blessing and hallowing it, being from the beginning of the world – say that the law had then place when the reason of the law took place.

(d) This is evident from Hebrews 4:3-9. The apostle there proves that there remains a Sabbath (or rest) to the people of God, into which they are to enter by faith, from this, that the Scripture speaks only of three sabbatisms or rests – one after the works of creation, another after the coming into Canaan (and David's words cannot be understood of the first, for that was over,[15] and so was the other); therefore there remaineth a rest for the people of God.[16]

Some allege against this that the patriarchs did not observe the Sabbath, because there is no mention made of it in the Scriptures. But this is no

---

12 Exodus 16:5. And it shall come to pass, that on the sixth day they shall prepare that which they bring in; and it shall be twice as much as they gather daily.

13 Exodus 16:23. And he said unto them, This is that which the LORD hath said, To morrow is the rest of the holy sabbath unto the LORD: bake that which ye will bake to day, and seethe that ye will seethe; and that which remaineth over lay up for you to be kept until the morning.

14 Exodus 16:26. Six days ye shall gather it, but on the seventh day, which is the sabbath, in it there shall be none.

15 Hebrews 4:3. We which have believed do enter into rest.

16 Hebrews 4:9. There remaineth therefore a rest to the people of God.

just argument, for at that rate we might as well conclude it was not observed all the time of the Judges, Samuel and Saul, for nowhere is it recorded in that history that they did. Yea, even if the patriarchs had not observed it, yet that could no more militate against the first institution of the Sabbath than their polygamy could militate against the first institution of marriage. But just as from the patriarchs sacrificing we infer the divine appointment of sacrifice, so from the institution of the Sabbath we may infer their keeping it. And their counting by weeks as Noah did[17] and Laban with Jacob[18] does not show it obscurely: for to what end did they use this computation, but that the Sabbath might be distinguished from other days? And the piety of the patriarchs persuades us that they observed that solemn day for worship – and if any day, what day but that day designed by God?

Sabbath – the first day of the week

As to the Sabbath of the first day of the week:

1. Consider the date of it. It was from the resurrection of Christ, to continue to the end of the world, for the days of the Gospel are the last days.

2. Consider how the Sabbath could be changed from the seventh to the first day of the week. The fourth commandment only commands a Sabbath to be kept, and that being one day in seven. As for the designation of the day, he that designated one day could designate another; and the substituting of a new day is the repealing of the old.

---

17   Genesis 8:10, 12. And he stayed yet other seven days; […] And he stayed yet other seven days.
18   Genesis 29:27-28. Fulfil her week, and we will give thee this also for the service which thou shalt serve with me yet seven other years. And Jacob did so, and fulfilled her week: and he gave him Rachel his daughter to wife also.

3. Consider wherefore this change was made. Upon account of the resurrection of Christ, wherein the work of man's redemption was completed.

4. Consider by what authority it was changed into the first day. The Sabbath was changed by divine authority from the seventh to the first day of the week, so that the Lord's Day is now by divine appointment the Christian Sabbath.

(a) The Sabbath of the first day of the week is prophesied of under the Old Testament (Psalm 118:24): 'This is the day which the LORD hath made,' namely the day of Christ's resurrection, when the stone which the builders rejected was made the head of the corner.[19] 'We will rejoice and be glad in it' (Psalm 118:24); that is, we will celebrate it as a day of rejoicing and thankfulness for the work of redemption. Compare Acts 4:10,11: 'Be it known unto you all, and to all the people of Israel, that by the name of Jesus Christ of Nazareth, whom ye crucified, whom God raised from the dead, even by him doth this man stand here before you whole. This is the stone which was set at nought of you builders, which is become the head of the corner.' It is possible that the following passage may refer to this matter (Ezekiel 43:27): 'And when these days are expired, it shall be, that upon the *eighth day,* and so forward, the priests shall make your burnt offerings upon the altar, and your peace offerings; and I will accept you, saith the Lord GOD.' And it may be called the eighth day, because the first day of the week now is the eighth in order from the creation. Also Isaiah 11:10: 'His rest shall be glorious.' As the Father's rest from the

---

19   Psalm 118:22. The stone which the builders refused is become the head stone of the corner. Matthew 21:42. Jesus saith unto them, Did ye never read in the scriptures, The stone which the builders rejected, the same is become the head of the corner: this is the Lord's doing, and it is marvellous in our eyes?
Mark 12:10. And have ye not read this scripture; The stone which the builders rejected is become the head of the corner?
Luke 20:17. And he beheld them, and said, What is this then that is written, The stone which the builders rejected, the same is become the head of the corner?

work of creation was glorious by the seventh day's rest, so the rest of the Son from the work of redemption was glorious by the first day's rest. On this day it was that the light was formed; so on this day did Christ the sun of righteousness, the true light, arise from the dark mansions of the grave with resplendent glory.

(b) This day is called 'the Lord's day' (Revelation 1:10). That this Lord's Day is the first day of the week is clear if you consider that John speaks of this day as a day known among Christians by that name. It could not be the Jewish Sabbath, for that is always called the Sabbath, and the Jewish Sabbaths were then repealed.[20] Neither could it mean any other day of the week wherein Christ specially manifested himself, for that would determine no day at all. And that this phrase infers a divine institution is evident from the matching phrase of the sacrament which is called *the Lord's Supper*.

(c) It is evident that there ought to be a Sabbath, and that from the creation till Christ's resurrection every seventh day was appointed by God himself. It is no less evident that the Sabbath is changed to the first day of the week, and that lawfully, because the Jewish Sabbath is repealed. Now, who could lawfully make this change but one who had divine authority? – the one who therefore is called Lord of the Sabbath.[21]

(d) It was the practice of the apostles and primitive Christians to observe the first day of the week for the Sabbath.[22] On this day the

---

20 Colossians 2:16-17. Let no man therefore judge you in meat, or in drink, or in respect of an holyday, or of the new moon, or of the sabbath days: which are a shadow of things to come; but the body is of Christ.

21 Mark 2:28. Therefore the Son of man is Lord also of the sabbath.

22 John 20:19. Then the same day at evening, being the first day of the week, when the doors were shut where the disciples were assembled for fear of the Jews, came Jesus and stood in the midst, and saith unto them, Peace be unto you.
    Acts 20:7. And upon the first day of the week, when the disciples came together to break bread, Paul preached unto them.

collection for the poor was made[23] and you know the apostles had from Christ what they delivered to the churches as to ordinances.[24]

5. The Lord, by glorious displays of his grace and Spirit has remarkably honoured this day in all ages of the Church; and by signal strokes from heaven has vindicated the honour of this day on the profaners of it. Remarkable instances of this may be seen in history, both at home and abroad.

Let us therefore sanctify this day as the day which God has appointed and blessed as a day of sacred rest in the Christian Church.

---

23   1 Corinthians 16:2. Upon the first day of the week let every one of you lay by him in store.
24   1 Corinthians 11:23. For I have received of the Lord that which also I delivered unto you, That the Lord Jesus the same night in which he was betrayed took bread.

Chapter 3

How is the Sabbath to be sanctified?

I come now to show you how the Sabbath is to be sanctified. The Catechism tells us, *It is to be sanctified by a holy resting all that day, even from such worldly employments and recreations as are lawful on other days; and spending the whole time in the public and private exercises of God's worship, except so much as is to be taken up in the works of necessity and mercy.*

Here I shall show what it is to sanctify the Sabbath, and what are the component parts of the sanctification of it. What is it to sanctify the Sabbath? The Sabbath Day is not capable of any sanctity or holiness except what is relative – that is, in respect of its use for holy rest or exercise. So:

(a) God has sanctified that day by setting it apart for holy uses, designing and appointing it in a special manner for his own worship and service.

(b) People must sanctify it by keeping it holy, spending that day in God's worship and service, for which God has set it apart, using it only for the uses unto which God has consecrated it.

What are the parts of the sanctification of the Sabbath? They are two – holy rest and holy exercise.

Sanctifying the Sabbath by a holy rest

The Sabbath is to be sanctified by a holy rest. Therefore it is called *a Sabbath,* i.e., a rest.

1. What are we to rest from?

On the Sabbath we must rest firstly from our worldly employments. God has given us six days for these, but his day must be kept free of them. 'In it thou shalt not do any work.' The works of our worldly calling have six days; those of our heavenly calling but one day. We must rest from the former so that we may apply ourselves to the latter. Now, such works are to be reckoned:

(a) We are to rest from all manual labour or servile employments tending to our worldly gain, as on the other days of the week, such as ploughing and sowing, bearing of burdens, driving of beasts to market, or exercising any part of one's calling (Nehemiah 13:15): 'In those days saw I in Judah some treading wine presses on the sabbath, and bringing in sheaves, and lading asses; as also wine, grapes, and figs, and all manner of burdens, which they brought into Jerusalem on the sabbath day: and I testified against them in the day wherein they sold victuals.'

(b) We are to rest from all study of liberal arts and sciences. The Sabbath is not a day for such exercises as reading history, studying sciences, etc. (Isaiah 58:13): 'If thou turn away thy foot from the sabbath, from doing thy pleasure on my holy day; and call the sabbath a delight, the holy of the LORD, honourable; and shalt honour him, not doing thine own ways, nor finding thine own pleasure, nor speaking thine own words.'

(c) We are to rest from all civil works, such as making of bargains, unnecessary journeying, and travelling to Monday markets on the Lord's Day, even though people wait on sermons or listen to sermons on the way. It is indeed the sin of those that do not change their market days when they occur on a Monday, and a sin in the government to tolerate it. But that will not justify those who comply with the temptation, seeing God has given us other days of the week. If they cannot reach their market after the Sabbath, they should go away before so that they may rest on the Sabbath wherever they are. 'See, for that the LORD hath given you the sabbath, therefore he giveth you on the sixth day the bread of two days; abide ye every man in his place, let no man go out of his place on the seventh day.' (Exodus 16:29).

Secondly, on the Sabbath we must rest from all worldly recreations, even though they are lawful on other days. It is not a day for carnal pleasures of any form, any more than it is for worldly employments. Our delights should be heavenly this day, not to please the flesh but the spirit; and sports, plays and pastimes are a gross profanation of the Sabbath.[25]

Now, this rest of the Sabbath from these things must be:

(a) A rest of the hands from them. The hands must rest, so that the heart may be duly exercised.

(b) A rest of the tongue. People should not give their orders for the week's work on the Lord's Day, nor converse about their worldly business.

(c) A rest of the head from thinking of it, and forming plans and contrivances about worldly affairs.

But here are excepted works of two sorts. Firstly, works of necessity, such as quenching a house on fire. Secondly, works of mercy, such as to save the life of a beast. 'And he said unto them, What man shall there be among you, that shall have one sheep, and if it fall into a pit on the sabbath day, will he not lay hold on it, and lift it out?' (Matthew 12:11).

These works of necessity and mercy may encompass:

(a) Good works, such as visiting the sick, relieving the poor, etc.

---

25   Isaiah 58:13-14. If thou turn away thy foot from the sabbath, from doing thy pleasure on my holy day; and call the sabbath a delight, the holy of the LORD, honourable; and shalt honour him, not doing thine own ways, nor finding thine own pleasure, nor speaking thine own words: then shalt thou delight thyself in the LORD; and I will cause thee to ride upon the high places of the earth, and feed thee with the heritage of Jacob thy father: for the mouth of the LORD hath spoken it.

(b) Works of decency, such as dressing the body with comely attire.

(c) Works of common honesty and humanity, such as saluting one another.[26]

(d) Works of necessary refreshment, such as dressing and taking of meat.

(e) Works having a necessary connection with and tendency to the worship of God, such as travelling on the Lord's Day to sermons.[27]

But in all these things it should be observed that the necessity should be real and not pretended, for it is not enough that the work cannot be done to such advantage on another day; for that might let out people on the Sabbath, if it be a windy day or so forth, in order to cut down their corn, which yet God has in a special manner provided against;[28] and that would have justified the sellers of fish whom Nehemiah dismissed.[29] And therefore I cannot think that the making of cheese on the Lord's Day can be accounted a work of necessity, lawful on that day; for the same might be said in the other cases as can be said in this case, namely that the corn may shake, the fishes may spoil, etc. Besides, people should take heed that bring not that necessity on themselves by timeously providing to prevent it. And when works of real necessity and mercy are to be done, they should be done not with a working day's frame of mind but with a Sabbath Day's frame.

---

26 1 Peter 3:8. Be ye all of one mind, having compassion one of another, love as brethren, be pitiful, be courteous.

27 2 Kings 4:22-23. Send me, I pray thee, one of the young men, and one of the asses, that I may run to the man of God, and come again. And he said, Wherefore wilt thou go to him to day? it is neither new moon, nor sabbath.

28 Exodus 34:21. Six days thou shalt work, but on the seventh day thou shalt rest: in earing time and in harvest thou shalt rest.

29 Nehemiah 13:16-19. There dwelt men of Tyre also therein, which brought fish, and all manner of ware, and sold on the sabbath unto the children of Judah, and in Jerusalem. Then I contended with the nobles of Judah, and said unto them, What evil thing is this that ye do, and profane the sabbath day? Did not your fathers thus, and did not our God bring all this evil upon us, and upon this city? yet ye bring more wrath upon Israel by profaning the sabbath.

2. Who are to rest on the Sabbath Day?

The command is very particular, both for people and for beasts.

(a) People are to rest on the Sabbath Day

(i) The heads of the family, the heads of the state, master and mistress – these are to give examples to others.

(ii) The children, *son, daughter*, they must not have their liberty to profane the Sabbath by playing any more than they would by working.

(iii) Servants, whose toil all the week may tempt them to misspend the Lord's Day. They must not be bidden to profane the Sabbath; and if they be bidden, they must obey God rather than man.

(iv) The stranger must not be allowed his liberty: we must not compliment away the honour of the Sabbath.

(b) Beasts are to rest on the Sabbath Day. Beasts must rest; not that the law reaches them for themselves, but for their owners, either because they require attendance at work, or put the case that they did not, yet it is the work which must not be done. This lets us see that where beasts may work on the Lord's Day unsupervised, yet it is not to be done.

3. What makes the Sabbath rest holy?

Respect to the command of God makes the rest holy.

Sanctifying the Sabbath by holy exercise

The Sabbath is to be sanctified by holy exercise.

1. Public exercises of God's worship,[30] such as hearing sermons,[31] prayer,[32] receiving of the sacraments, where there is occasion,[33] and singing of psalms.[34]

---

30   Isaiah 66:23. And it shall come to pass [...] from one Sabbath to another, shall all flesh come to worship before me, saith the LORD.

2. Private exercise of worship, alone and in our families.[35] Neither of these must jostle out the other. God has joined them: let us not put them asunder.

And these duties are to be done with a special elevation of heart on the Sabbath Day; they ought to be performed with a frame suiting the Sabbath.[36]

(a) Grace must be stirred up to exercise, otherwise the Sabbath will be a burden. Grace will be at its height in heaven, and the Sabbath is an emblem of heaven.[37]

(b) The heart should be withdrawn from all earthly things, and intent upon the duty of the day. We must leave the ass at the foot of the mountain, that we may converse with God.

(c) Love and admiration are special ingredients here. The two great works of creation and redemption, which we are particularly called to remember on the Lord's Day, are calculated to excite our love and admiration.

(d) We should have a peculiar delight in the day and the duties of it, exchanging our lawful pleasures on other days with spiritual pleasures on this day.

---

31 Luke 4:16. And he came to Nazareth, where he had been brought up: and, as his custom was, he went into the synagogue on the sabbath day, and stood up for to read.

32 Acts 16:13-14. And he came to Nazareth, where he had been brought up: and, as his custom was, he went into the synagogue on the sabbath day, and stood up for to read.

33 Acts 20:7. Upon the first day of the week, when the disciples came together to break bread, Paul preached unto them.

34 Psalm 92, title. A psalm or song for the sabbath day.

35 Leviticus 23:3. Six days shall work be done: but the seventh day is the sabbath of rest, an holy convocation; ye shall do no work therein: it is the sabbath of the LORD in all your dwellings.

36 Isaiah 58:13. If thou turn away thy foot from the sabbath, from doing thy pleasure on my holy day; and call the sabbath a delight, the holy of the LORD, honourable; and shalt honour him, not doing thine own ways, nor finding thine own pleasure, nor speaking thine own words.

37 Revelation 1:10. I was in the Spirit on the Lord's day.

The holy rest must be combined with the holy exercises

The rest without holy exercise is not sufficient.

1. The Sabbath rest resembles that of heaven, which is a rest without a rest, wherein the soul is most busy and active, serving the Lord without weariness.

2. If it were enough to rest without holy exercise, we would be obliged to sanctify the Sabbath no more than beasts, which only rest that day.

3. The rest enjoined is not commanded for itself, but for the holy exercises of the day.

Now, it is the whole day that is thus to be spent in rest with holy exercise – i.e., the natural day. Not that people are bound to be in these exercises without intermission all the twenty-four hours, for God has not made the Sabbath to be a burden to man, but that we should continue God's work as we do our own on other days, where we are allowed necessary rest and refreshment by sleep in the night.

Application

Remember the Sabbath Day to keep it holy. This note is put upon it for the following two reasons.

1. Because of the great weight of the thing, the Sabbath being the bond of all religion. It is God's day for dealing with the soul, wherein his people may expect to be furnished for all the week.

2. Because we are very apt to forget it.[38] There is less light of nature for this than other commands. It restrains our liberty in those things that we do all the week. And Satan, knowing the importance of it for our souls,

---

38   Ezekiel 22:26. Her priests [...] have hid their eyes from my sabbaths, and I am profaned among them.

that it is a day of blessing, sets us on to forget it. If you would then sanctify the Sabbath, remember the Sabbath Day in these three ways:

(a) Remember it before it comes; on the last day of the week, on the Saturday's evening, laying by work in good time to prepare for it.[39]

(b) Remember it when it is come; rise early on the Sabbath morning.[40] The morning has enough ado. Worship God secretly and privately; prepare yourselves for ordinances, wrestle with God for his presence in them, that he may graciously assist the minister in preaching, and may graciously assist you in hearing and may bless the Word to you. Remember it whilst it is going on, that it is God's day, a day of blessing, and ply diligently the work of the day, not only in time of the public work, but after, till the day be finished.

(c) Remember it when it is over, to see what good you have got by it; to bless him for any smiles of his face, or manifestations of his grace; and to mourn over your failures, and apply to the blood of Christ for pardon and cleansing.

---

39 Luke 23:54. And that day was the preparation, and the sabbath drew on.
40 Psalm 92:1-2. It is a good thing [...] to shew forth thy lovingkindness in the morning.

Chapter 4

What is forbidden in this command?

I proceed to show what is forbidden in the fourth commandment. We are told in the Catechism that it 'forbiddeth the omission or careless performance of the duties required, and the profaning the day by idleness, or doing that which is in itself sinful, or by unnecessary thoughts, words, or works, about worldly employments or recreations'.

Omission of Sabbath duties

This commandment is broken by omission of the duties required on this day, whether in whole or in part. Many of the Sabbath duties are the duties of every day; but the omission of them, which is always criminal, is more so on this day, because on it we are specially called to them. We sin against this command, then, when we neglect the public or private exercises of God's worship.

1. Not remembering the Sabbath, before it comes, to prepare of it; entertaining a carnal, worldly frame of spirit on the night before, not laying aside work in good time and composing our hearts for the approaching Sabbath – far more when people continue at their work later that night than ordinary, getting as near the borders of the Sabbath as they can.

2. Neglecting the duties of the Sabbath morning; particularly:
   (a) The duty of meditation. Those that are in the spirit on the Lord's Day, their spirits will be busy, elevated to heavenly things, and conversing with heaven. The two great works of creation and redemp-

tion require our thoughts particularly on that day[41] and we must needs be guilty when, while God has set these great marks before us, we do not aim to hit them. Has not God made it a day of blessing? Should not we then consider our wants, miseries and needs, and sharpen our appetites after that food that is set before us in ordinances on that day?

(b) Secret prayer. The Sabbath morning is a special time for wrestling with God, confessing, petitioning and giving thanks. Then there should be wrestling for the blessing on the day of blessing. And the neglect of it is a very bad beginning for that good day. When will they come to God's door who will not come then?[42]

(c) Family exercise. This command has a special respect to family religion. As God will have the family to mind and see to their own work on the six days, so he calls them to mind his work together on the Sabbath. Every family is to be a church, especially on the Lord's Day. And if people came with their hearts warmed from family duties to the public, they would speed [prosper].

3. Neglect of the public exercises of God's worship.[43] By this neglect the Sabbath is profaned. The public ordinances on the Lord's Day, whatever else they do, they keep up a standard for Christ in the world; and to slight them is the way to fill the world with atheism and profaneness. As it would be the sin of ministers not to administer them, so it is the sin of people not to attend on them. But O how does this profanation abound, by unnecessary absenting from public ordinances! It is not enough to spend the time in private. God requires both; and the one must not

---

41   Psalm 92:5. O LORD, how great are thy works! and thy thoughts are very deep.

42   Psalm 92:1-2. It is a good thing to give thanks unto the LORD, and to sing praises unto thy name, O most High: to shew forth thy lovingkindness in the morning, and thy faithfulness every night.

43   Hebrews 10:25. Not forsaking the assembling of ourselves together, as the manner of some is; but exhorting one another: and so much the more, as ye see the day approaching.

jostle out the other. Nothing should be admitted as an excuse in this, but what will bear weight when the conscience is sifted before God.

4. Neglecting the duties of the day when the public work is over. The Sabbath is not over when the public work is over. When we go home to our houses we must keep the Sabbath there too.[44] It ought not to be an idle time. You ought to retire by yourselves and meditate on what you have heard, on your behaviour at the public ordinances, and be humbled for your failings. You ought to confer together about the Word, renew your calling on God in secret and in your families, and spend what remains of the day in various holy exercises.

Careless performances of Sabbath duties

The Sabbath is profaned by a careless performance of the duties required. Though we perform the duties themselves, we may profane the Sabbath by the way of managing them. Now, it is a careless performance to perform them:

1. Hypocritically, while the body is exercised in Sabbath work, but the heart does not go along with it.[45]

2. Carnally, in an earthly frame of spirit, the heart savouring nothing of heaven, but still of the world. Hence are so many distracting thoughts about worldly things, that the heart cannot be intent on the duty of the day.[46]

---

44 Leviticus 23:3. Six days shall work be done: but the seventh day is the sabbath of rest, an holy convocation; ye shall do no work therein: it is the sabbath of the LORD in all your dwellings.

45 Matthew 15:7-8. Ye hypocrites, well did Esaias prophesy of you, saying, This people draweth nigh unto me with their mouth, and honoureth me with their lips; but their heart is far from me.

46 Amos 8:5-6. When will the new moon be gone, that we may sell corn? and the sabbath, that we may set forth wheat, making the ephah small, and the shekel great, and falsifying the balances

3. Heartlessly and coldly. The Sabbath should be called a delight; a special vigour and alacrity is required to Sabbath duties. But O how flat, heartless, dead and dull are we for the most part! – so that many are quite out of their element on the Lord's Day, and never come to themselves or any alacrity of spirit till the Sabbath be over and they return to their business.

4. To perform them with a weariness of them or in in them.[47] Alas! Is not the Sabbath the most wearisome day of all the week to many? The rest of the Sabbath is more burdensome than the toil of other days. How will such take with heaven, where there is an eternal rest, an everlasting Sabbath? This is a contempt of God and of his day.

Idleness on Sabbath

The Sabbath is profaned by idleness. God has made the Sabbath a rest, but not a mere rest. He never allows idleness. On the weekdays we must not be idle, or else we misspend our own time; on the Lord's Day we must not be idle, or else we misspend and profane God's time. Thus the Sabbath is idled away and profaned:

1. By unnecessary unseasonable sleeping in that day: lying long in the Sabbath morning, going soon to bed that night, to cut God's day as short as may be, and much more sleeping in any other time of the day, to pass the time.

2. By vain gadding abroad on the Lord's Day, through the fields or gathering together about the doors, to idle away the time in company. It is very necessary that people keep indoors on the Lord's Day as much as

---

by deceit? That we may buy the poor for silver, and the needy for a pair of shoes; yea, and sell the refuse of the wheat?

47 Malachi 1:13. Ye said also, Behold, what a weariness is it! and ye have snuffed at it, saith the LORD of hosts; and ye brought that which was torn, and the lame, and the sick; thus ye brought an offering: should I accept this of your hand? saith the LORD.

they can; and if necessity or circumstances call them forth, that they carry their Sabbath's work with them.

3. By vain and idle discourse or thoughts. We must give an account of every idle word spoken on any day, far more for those spoken on the Lord's Day, which are doubly sinful.

Sinning on Sabbath

The Sabbath is profaned by doing that which is in itself sinful. To do those things on the Lord's Day, that ought not to be done any day, is a sin which is highly aggravated [made particularly heinous]. Thus the Sabbath is profaned by people discouraging others from attending ordinances instead of attending them themselves; swearing or cursing on that day instead of praising God. The better the day, the worse is the deed. How fearful must their doom be who await that time for their wicked pranks, such as some dishonest servants and other naughty [wicked] persons, who choose the time that others are at church for their hidden works of dishonesty, because then they get most secrecy? And indeed the devil is very busy that way, and has brought some on to commit such things on the Sabbath Day as have brought them to a bad end.

Worldly employments and recreations on Sabbath

The Sabbath is profaned by unnecessary thoughts, words or works, about worldly employments or recreations. The Sabbath is profaned in the following ways:

1. By carnal recreations, in no way necessary or suitable to the work of the Sabbath, such as all carnal pleasures, sports, plays and pastimes.[48]

2. By following of worldly employments on that day, working or going about ordinary business, except in cases of necessity and mercy.[49] Though, where real necessity or mercy is, it is an abuse of that day to forbear such things, as sometimes the Jews did who, being attacked on the Lord's Day, would not defend themselves.

3. By unnecessary thoughts or discourse about them; for that day is a day of rest from them every way, and we should neither think of them nor talk about them.

O let us be deeply humbled before the Lord under the sense of our profanations of the Sabbath! For who can plead innocent here? We are all guilty in some shape or other, and need to flee to the atoning blood of Jesus for the expiation of this and all our other sins.

---

48   Isaiah 58:13. If thou turn away thy foot from the sabbath, from doing thy pleasure on my holy day; and call the sabbath a delight, the holy of the LORD, honourable; and shalt honour him, not doing thine own ways, nor finding thine own pleasure, nor speaking thine own words.

49   Matthew 24:20. Pray ye that your flight be not in the winter, neither on the sabbath day.

45

Chapter 5

What are the reasons annexed to the command?

I come now to consider the reasons annexed to the fourth commandment. And these, according to the Catechism, are, 'God's allowing us six
days of the week for our own employments, his challenging a special
propriety in the seventh, his own example, and his blessing the Sabbath
Day'.

This command God has enforced by four reasons.

The equity of the command

The first reason is taken from the equity of this command. God has
allowed us six days out of seven for our own business, and has reserved
but one for himself. In dividing our time between himself and us, he has
made our share great: six for one. Consider the force of this reason:

(a) We have time enough to serve ourselves in the six days, and shall
we not serve God on the seventh? They that will not be satisfied with
six, would as little be satisfied with sixteen. But carnal hearts are like a
bed of sand to devour that which is holy.

(b) We have time enough to tire ourselves on the six days in our own
employments; it is a kindness that we are obliged to rest on the Lord's
Day. Our interest is our duty, and our duty is our interest. It is a kindness to our bodies and souls too. And shall we not be engaged by it to
sanctify the Sabbath?

(c) There is time enough to raise the appetite for the Sabbath. It
comes so seldom, though so sweet to the exercised soul, that we may

long for it and rejoice at the return of it. It is sad if six days' interval cannot make us find our stomach.

(d) God might have allowed us but one day, and taken six to himself. Who could have quarrelled the Lord of time? Has he reserved but one for six, and shall we grudge it him? The sentence of David in the parable against the rich man that took away the poor man's one ewe lamb is applicable here: 'The man that hath done this thing shall surely die: and he shall restore the lamb fourfold,' etc. (2 Samuel 12:5-6).

God has reserved this day as the Lord's Day

The second reason is taken from God's challenging a special propriety [exclusive right] in the Sabbath Day: 'But the seventh day is the sabbath of the Lord thy God'. All days are his, but this is his in a peculiar manner.[50] He has set a mark on it for himself, to be reserved for himself. Consider the force of this reason:

(a) If we have a God, it is reasonable that God should have a time set apart for his service, 'the Sabbath of the Lord thy God'. The heathens had days set apart for the honour of their idols; though the dumb idols could not demand them, yet they gave them. Papists have days set apart for saints, who are to them a sort of gods, though some of them have forbidden it, just as Paul has done. And will you not keep holy the Sabbath of the Lord thy God?

(b) It is sacrilege, the worst of theft, to profane the Sabbath Day. It is a robbing of God, a stealing from him of time that is consecrated to him, and that is dangerous.[51] We justly blame the churches of Rome and England for robbing people of a great many days which God has given us; but how may we blame ourselves for robbing God of the day he has kept from us and taken to himself! Alas! Our zeal for God is far below

---

50 Revelation 1:10. I was in the Spirit on the Lord's day.
51 Proverbs 20:25. It is a snare to the man who devoureth that which is holy.

our zeal for ourselves. They stick to their saints' days, but how weary are we of our God's days?[52]

God set an example of resting from his work of creation

The third reason is taken from God's example who, though he could have perfected the world in a moment, yet spent six days in it – and only six days – resting the seventh, taking a complacency [pleasure] in the work of his own hand; and this is an example to be imitated by us. Consider the force of this reason:

(a) God's example proposed for imitation is a most binding rule: 'Be ye followers of God' (Ephesians 5:1). What God does is best done, and we must labour to write after his copy.

(b) The profaning of the Sabbath is a most eminent and signal contempt of God and of his works. Did God rest on the Sabbath, taking a complacency [pleasure] in the six days' works? Our not doing so is an undervaluing of what God so highly esteemed, slighting of what he so much prized, and consequently a contempt of himself and his works too.

God has appointed it as a day of blessing to us

The fourth reason is taken from his blessing the Sabbath Day. His blessing of that day is his blessing it as a means of blessing us in the keeping of it. It indicates:

(a) The Lord's putting a peculiar honour on it beyond all other days. It is 'the holy of the Lord, honourable' (Isaiah 58:13). The King of heaven has made it the queen of days. Therefore it should be our question, 'What shall be done to that day the King delights to

---

52   Malachi 3:8. Will a man rob God? Yet ye have robbed me.

honour?' Let us beware of levelling that with common things which God has advanced so far above them.

(b) That the Lord has set it apart for a spiritual blessing to his people, so that in the sanctification of that day we may look for a blessing[53] – nay, that the Lord will multiply his blessings on that day more on his people than any other days wherein they seek it. So that, as the Lord requires more on that day than on any other days, he also gives more.

(c) That the Lord will make it even a spring of temporal blessings. He will not let the day of blessing be a curse to people in their temporal affairs. They shall be at no loss in their worldly things by the Sabbath rest (Leviticus 25:20-22). Conscientious keepers of the Sabbath will be found to thrive as well in other ways as those who are not. The force of this reason is: Firstly, God's honour by keeping of that day, that we may get his blessings on it showered down upon us. So that the profanation of the Sabbath is like profane Esau's rejecting the blessing. Secondly, it is our own interest. Is it a special day for blessing, and shall we not observe it? It is an unworthy mistake to look on the Sabbath as so much lost time. No time is so gainful as a Sabbath observed in a holy manner. And indeed the great reason of the profaning of the Sabbath may be found to lie in the following three matters:

(i) In carnality and worldly-mindedness. The Sabbath is no delight to many. Why? Because heaven would be no heaven to them, for they savour not the things of God. The heart that is drowned in the cares or pleasures of the world all week long, is as hard to get in a Sabbath frame as wet wood is to take fire.

---

53   Isaiah 56:6-7. Also the sons of the stranger, that join themselves to the LORD, to serve him, and to love the name of the LORD, to be his servants, every one that keepeth the sabbath from polluting it, and taketh hold of my covenant; even them will I bring to my holy mountain, and make them joyful in my house of prayer: their burnt offerings and their sacrifices shall be accepted upon mine altar; for mine house shall be called an house of prayer for all people.

(ii) Insensibleness of their need of spiritual blessings. They are not sensible of their wants, and hence they despise the blessing. He that has nothing to buy or sell can stay at home on the market day, and the full soul does not care for God's day.

(iii) The not believing of the blessing of that day. They that think they may come as good speed any day in the duties of the day as on the Lord's Day, no wonder that they count God's day and the duties of it as common.

Chapter 6

Practical application

Let me exhort you then to beware of profaning the Sabbath. Learn to keep it holy. And therefore I would call you here to eight duties.

1. Remember the Sabbath Day before it comes, to prepare for it, and let your eye be on it before the week is past. Cease from your worldly employment in good time, and do not go near the borders of the Lord's Day, and strive to get your hearts in a frame suitable to the exercises of this holy day.

2. Make conscience of attending the public ordinances and waiting on God in his own house on his own day. Do not loiter away the Lord's Day at home unnecessarily, seeing the Lord makes an appointment to meet his people there. This will bring leanness to your own soul, and grief of heart to him who bears the Lord's message to you.

3. Before you come to the public exercises, spend the morning in secret and private exercises, particularly in prayer, reading and meditation, remembering how much your success depends upon suitable preparation. Put off your shoes before you tread the holy ground.

4. Do not make your attendance on the public ordinances a by-hand [casual] work and a means for carrying on your worldly affairs. If you come to the church to meet with somebody and to discourse or make appointments about your worldly business, it will be a wonder if you meet with the Lord. If you travel on the Lord's Day and take a preaching by the way, it may well cheat your blinded consciences; it will not be pleasing to God, for it makes his service to stand merely in the second

place, while your main end is what concerns your temporal affairs. Among the Jews no man might make a house or a synagogue a thoroughfare. And beware of common discourse between sermons, which is too much practised among professing people.

5. When you come home from the public ordinances, let it be your care, both by the way and at home, to meditate or converse about spiritual things and what you have heard. Retire and examine yourselves as to what you have gained, and do not be as the unclean beasts which chew not the cud. Let masters of families take account of their children and servants how they have profited; let them catechise and instruct them in the principles of religion, and exhort them to piety.

6. When you are necessarily detained from the public ordinances let your hearts be there,[54] and do not turn that to sin which in itself is not your sin. And strive to spend the Lord's Day in private and secret worship, looking to the Lord for making up your deficiencies. As for those that tie themselves to men's service, without a due regard to having opportunities to hear the Lord's Word, their wages are bought dearly and they have little respect to God or their own souls. And I think tender Christians will be loath to pledge themselves in this way. But, alas, few masters or servants look further than the work and wages in their engaging together! This is a sad evidence that religion is at a low ebb.

7. Do not cut the Sabbath short. The Church of Rome has half holy days. God never appointed any such – it is one whole day. Alas! It is a sad thing to see how the Lord's Day is consumed, as if people would make up the loss of a day out of Saturday night and Monday morning, which they do by cutting short the Lord's Day.

---

54   Psalm 63:1-2. O God, thou art my God; early will I seek thee: my soul thirsteth for thee, my flesh longeth for thee in a dry and thirsty land, where no water is; to see thy power and thy glory, so as I have seen thee in the sanctuary.

8. Labour to be in a Sabbath Day's frame. Let the thoughts of worldly business be far from you, and far more let worldly words and works be far from you. To press this, consider the following:

(a) It is God's command, whereby he tries your love to him. This day is as the forbidden fruit. Who does not condemn Adam and Eve for eating of it? O do not profane it any manner of way!

(b) Heaven will be an everlasting Sabbath, and our conversation should be heaven-like. If we grudge the Lord one day in seven, how will we digest an eternity? We are ready to complain that we are toiled with the world; why then do we not enter into his rest?

(c) The great advantage of sanctifying the Lord's Day. He has made it a day of blessing. It is God's day for trading with the soul, and keeps up the heart of many through the week while they think of its approach.

(d) You will bring wrath on you if you do not sanctify the Sabbath. God may plague you with temporal, spiritual and eternal plagues. Many begin with this sin of profaning the Lord's Day, and it brings them at length to an ill hour, both in this world and in that which is to come.

Part 2

The Shorter Catechism explained
by questions and answers

James Fisher, Glasgow

Shorter Catechism question 57

Which is the fourth commandment?

The fourth commandment is, 'Remember the sabbath day, to keep it holy. Six days shalt thou labour, and do all thy work: but the seventh day is the sabbath of the LORD thy God: in it thou shalt not do any work, thou, nor thy son, nor thy daughter, thy manservant, nor thy maidservant, nor thy cattle, nor thy stranger that is within thy gates: for in six days the LORD made heaven and earth, the sea, and all that in them is, and rested the seventh day: wherefore the LORD blessed the sabbath day, and hallowed it.'
Exodus 20:8-11

Shorter Catechism question 58

What is required in the fourth commandment?

The fourth commandment requireth the keeping holy to God such set times as he hath appointed in his word; expressly one whole day in seven, to be a holy sabbath to himself.[55]

Q. 1. To what about the worship of God has this command a reference?

A. It refers to the special time of God's worship.

Q. 2. Is the time of God's worship left arbitrary to the will of man?

A. No; we are to keep 'holy to God such set times as he hath appointed in his Word'.

Q. 3. Why should 'such set times' be kept holy, and no other?

A. Because God is the sovereign Lord of our time, and has the sole power and authority to direct how it should be improved.

Q. 4. What is meant by the 'set times' mentioned in the answer?

A. The stated feasts and holy convocations for religious worship, instituted under the ceremonial law, which the church of the Jews was obliged to observe during that dispensation (Leviticus 23).

Q. 5. Is there any warrant for anniversary or stated holidays [holy days] now, under the New Testament?

A. No; these under the Old, being abrogated by the death and resur-

---

55 Deuteronomy 5:12-14. *Keep the sabbath day* to sanctify it, *as the LORD thy God hath commanded thee.* Six days thou shalt labour, and do all thy work: *but the seventh day is the sabbath of the LORD thy God: in it thou shalt not do any work,* thou, nor thy son, nor thy daughter, nor thy manservant, nor thy maidservant, nor thine ox, nor thine ass, nor any of thy cattle, nor thy stranger that is within thy gates; that thy manservant and thy maidservant may rest as well as thou.

rection of Christ, there is neither precept nor example in Scripture for any of the yearly holidays observed by Papists and others: on the contrary, all such days are condemned in bulk.[56]

Q. 6. What crimes does the observance of them import [signify]?

A. The observance of them imports no less than an impeachment of the institutions of God concerning his worship, as if they were imperfect, and an encroachment upon the liberty wherewith Christ has made his church and people free.[57]

Q. 7. What is the special and stated time which God has 'expressly' appointed in his word to be kept holy?

A. 'One whole day in seven, to be a holy Sabbath to himself.'

Q. 8. What is meant by a 'whole day'?

A. A whole natural day, consisting of twenty-four hours.

Q. 9. What do you understand by 'one whole day in seven'?

A. A seventh part of our weekly time; or one complete day, either after or before six days' labour.

Q. 10. When should we begin and end this day?

A. We should measure it just as we do other days, from midnight to midnight, without alienating [transferring] any part of it to our own works.

Q. 11. Are not sleeping and eating on the Sabbath Day our own works?

A. If these refreshments of nature are in moderation, and to the glory of God on the Sabbath, they are not properly our own works, because they are necessary to strengthen our bodies for religious exercises.

---

56 Galatians 4:10. Ye observe days, and months, and times, and years.
   Colossians 2:16-17. Let no man therefore judge you in meat, or in drink, or in respect of an holyday, or of the new moon, or of the sabbath days: which are a shadow of things to come.
57 Colossians 2:20. Wherefore if ye be dead with Christ from the rudiments of the world, why, as though living in the world, are ye subject to ordinances?

Q. 12. What is the significance of the word 'Sabbath'?
A. It is a Hebrew word, signifying rest, as it is interpreted (Hebrews 4:9): 'There remaineth therefore a rest (margin: keeping of a Sabbath) to the people of God.'

Q. 13. Is Sunday a proper or fit name for this day?
A. Although it cannot charitably be supposed that many who use this term have any knowledge of it, or pay the smallest regard to the idolatrous rise of this name or the names assigned to the other days of the week, yet it were to be wished that all Christians would call this holy day by one or other of its Scripture designations.

Q. 14. May it not continue to be called Sabbath now, as well as under the Old Testament?
A. Yes; in regard our Lord himself calls it by this name (Matthew 24:20): 'Pray ye that your flight be not in the winter, neither on the sabbath day.'

Q. 15. But is not our Lord speaking there of the Jewish and not of the Christian Sabbath?
A. He is speaking of the Christian Sabbath only; for he is speaking of the flight which should happen at the destruction of Jerusalem, which did not take place till about forty years after the Jewish Sabbath was abolished, and the Christian Sabbath come in its room.

Q. 16. Why is it called a 'holy Sabbath'?
A. Because it was consecrated and set apart by God himself for his own worship and service.

Q. 17. Is there any other day holy but the Sabbath alone?
A. Other days may be occasionally employed in the worship of God, according to providential calls thereunto, yet there is no other day morally and perpetually holy but the Sabbath only.

Q. 18. Is the Sabbath instrumentally, or is the time itself of the Sabbath, an instrument and means (as the word and sacraments are) of conveying spiritual grace?

A. Not at all; for the time of the Sabbath is only a holy season, wherein God is pleased to bless his people, more ordinarily than at other times;[58] still reserving to himself the prerogative of communicating his grace at other times likewise, as he shall see meet.[59]

Q. 19. Is the fourth commandment founded on the light of nature, or upon positive institution?

A. It is founded partly on both.

Q. 20. What part of this commandment is it that is founded entirely on nature's light, or is what they call moral-natural?

A. The substance of it, namely, that as God is to be worshipped, so some stated time should be set apart for that end.

Q. 21. What part of it is founded on positive institution, or is what

---

58 John 20:19-24. Then the same day at evening, being the first day of the week, when the doors were shut where the disciples were assembled for fear of the Jews, came Jesus and stood in the midst, and saith unto them, Peace be unto you. And when he had so said, he shewed unto them his hands and his side. Then were the disciples glad, when they saw the Lord. Then said Jesus to them again, Peace be unto you: as my Father hath sent me, even so send I you. And when he had said this, he breathed on them, and saith unto them, Receive ye the Holy Ghost: whose soever sins ye remit, they are remitted unto them; and whose soever sins ye retain, they are retained. But Thomas, one of the twelve, called Didymus, was not with them when Jesus came.

59 John 21:15-18. So when they had dined, Jesus saith to Simon Peter, Simon, son of Jonas, lovest thou me more than these? He saith unto him, Yea, Lord; thou knowest that I love thee. He saith unto him, Feed my lambs. He saith to him again the second time, Simon, son of Jonas, lovest thou me? He saith unto him, Yea, Lord; thou knowest that I love thee. He saith unto him, Feed my sheep. He saith unto him the third time, Simon, son of Jonas, lovest thou me? Peter was grieved because he said unto him the third time, Lovest thou me? And he said unto him, Lord, thou knowest all things; thou knowest that I love thee. Jesus saith unto him, Feed my sheep. Verily, verily, I say unto thee, When thou wast young, thou girdedst thyself, and walkedst whither thou wouldest: but when thou shalt be old, thou shalt stretch forth thy hands, and another shall gird thee, and carry thee whither thou wouldest not.

they call moral-positive?

A. That one proportion of time should be observed for God's worship and service rather than another, namely, that it should be a seventh rather than a third, fourth, fifth, or sixth part of our weekly time.

Q. 22. Why do you call this a positive institution?

A. Because the observance of one day in seven for a Sabbath flows from the sovereign will of God in appointing it, and could never have been observed more than any other part of time merely by the force of nature's light.

Q. 23. Why do you call it moral-positive?

A. Because though the law appointing the precise time of the Sabbath be positive, yet the reason of the law (plainly implied in the law itself, namely, that Divine Wisdom saw it most equal and meet that man having six, God should have a seventh day to himself) is moral.

Q. 24. Wherein then consists the morality of the fourth commandment?

A. In keeping holy to God any seventh day he shall be pleased to appoint.

Q. 25. What is meant by the seventh day mentioned in the commandment?

A. Not only the seventh in order from the creation, but any other seventh part of our weekly time as God shall determine.

Q. 26. How does this appear from the words of the command itself?

A. In the beginning of the commandment it is not said 'Remember the seventh day' (namely in order from the creation) but 'Remember the sabbath day, to keep it holy.' Just so in the end of the command the words are not 'The Lord blessed the seventh day' but 'The Lord blessed the sabbath day and hallowed it.'

Q. 27. How do you prove the observance of 'one whole day in seven' for a holy Sabbath to the Lord to be of a moral and perpetual obligation?

A. From the time of the first institution of the Sabbath, from its being placed in the Decalogue or summary of moral precepts, and from there being nothing originally ceremonial or typical [symbolic] in the scope or substance of it.

Q. 28. When was the Sabbath first instituted?

A. The will of God that some stated time should be set apart for his worship was written with the rest of the commandments upon man's heart at his first creation, and God's resting from all his works on the first seventh day, his blessing and sanctifying thereof,[60] were sufficient evidences of the will of God to mankind that they should observe every seventh day thereafter till God should be pleased to alter it.

Q. 29. How is the morality of the Sabbath evinced from the first institution of it?

A. Being instituted while Adam was in innocence, and consequently before all types and ceremonies respecting an atonement for sin, and being appointed him upon a moral ground, without any particular reference to an innocent state more than any other, it must therefore be of perpetual obligation.

Q. 30. What was the moral ground upon which the Sabbath was appointed unto Adam?

A. It was this, that infinite wisdom saw it meet for God's glory, and needful for man's good, that man have one day in the week for more immediate and special converse with God.

---

60   Genesis 2:1-3. Thus the heavens and the earth were finished, and all the host of them. And on the seventh day God ended his work which he had made; and he rested on the seventh day from all his work which he had made. And God blessed the seventh day, and sanctified it: because that in it he had rested from all his work which God created and made.

Q. 31. What need was there for Adam in innocence, being perfectly holy, to have one day by another [set apart from another] for more immediate converse with God?

A. That in this he might be like unto God, who set him an example of holy working six days and of a holy resting on the seventh.

Q. 32. Could Adam's mind be equally intent upon the immediate worship of God, when about his ordinary employment in dressing the garden, as on a day set apart for that purpose?

A. No; for though there could be no interruption of his happiness and fellowship with God when dressing the garden as he was a perfect creature, yet, being at the same time a finite creature, his mind, while he was about that employment, could not be so intense upon the immediate worship of God as it would be on a day set apart for that purpose; therefore it was fit he should have such a day, that in it he might have uninterrupted freedom in the immediate contemplation and enjoyment of his Maker, without any avocation [distraction] from worldly things.

Q. 33. What may be inferred from this, in favour of the morality of the Sabbath?

A. That if Adam in innocence needed a Sabbath for the more immediate service and solemn worship of God, much more do we, who are sinful creatures and so immersed in worldly cares, need such a day.

Q. 34. Did the religious observance of the Sabbath take place immediately after the creation, or not till the publishing of the law at Mount Sinai?

A. It took place at and from the first seventh day after the creation, for God's blessing and sanctifying of the Sabbath is related as a thing actually done at that time, and not as a thing to be done upwards of two thousand years afterwards.[61]

Q. 35. How can the observance of the Sabbath be said to have taken place immediately after the creation, when the Scripture is wholly silent about the observance of it till the time of Moses?

A. It might as well be argued, that the Sabbath was not observed after Moses' time, during the government of the Judges (which, according to Acts 13:20, was 'about the space of four hundred and fifty years'), there being no mention of the church observing a Sabbath during the whole of that long period: and yet it cannot be supposed, that such godly men as the Judges were, would suffer the observance of the Sabbath to go into entire disuse.

Q. 36. Is there any evidence from Scripture that the Israelites knew the observance of the Sabbath to be a moral duty before the publication of the law from Mount Sinai?

A. Yes; for when the manna was first given them, before they came to Mount Sinai, Moses speaks of the Sabbath, as a day well known to them (Exodus 16:23): 'Tomorrow is the rest of the holy sabbath unto the Lord.'

Q. 37. How may the morality of the Sabbath be demonstrated from its situation in the Decalogue, or Ten Commandments?

A. It is placed in the midst of moral precepts, and must therefore be of the same nature and kind with them. It has the same dignity and honour put upon it that the other nine commandments have; for it was, with them, proclaimed by the mouth of God in the hearing of all Israel, twice written upon tables of stone by the finger of God, and with them lodged within the ark; none of which privileges were conferred upon the cere-

---

61   Genesis 2:3. And God blessed the seventh day, and sanctified it: because that in it he had rested from all his work which God created and made.

monial law, and consequently the fourth commandment must be of the same perpetual obligation as the other moral precepts.[62]

Q. 38. Was there any thing typical of Christ in the original institution of the Sabbath?

A. It is impossible there could be; for Adam in innocence being under a covenant of works, had no need of Christ or the revelation of him by types; no, not to confirm him in that covenant.[63]

Q. 39. What would have been the consequence, if the Sabbath had been originally and essentially typical?

A. If so, then it would have been abolished upon the death of Christ, and there would be no more remembrance of it than of the new moons and jubilees; which is, indeed, what they who argue against the morality of the Sabbath seem much to desire.

Q. 40. Were not the Israelites commanded to keep the Sabbath Day in memory of their deliverance out of Egypt, which was typical of our redemption by Christ?

A. Yes; their deliverance out of Egypt was annexed, at Mount Sinai, as a superadded ground for the observance of that particular seventh day which God appointed to be kept immediately after the creation.[64] For which reason, this particular seventh day was abolished at the resurrection of Christ; but still the seventh part of weekly time fixed by God at the beginning, as the substance of this commandment, remained unchangeably moral.

Q. 41. Will it follow that the substance of this commandment is

---

62 James 2:10. For whosoever shall keep the whole law, and yet offend in one point, he is guilty of all.

63 Galatians 3:12. And the law is not of faith: but, The man that doeth them shall live in them.

64 Deuteronomy 5:15. And remember that thou wast a servant in the land of Egypt, and that the LORD thy God brought thee out thence through a mighty hand and by a stretched out arm: therefore the LORD thy God commanded thee to keep the sabbath day.

ceremonial, because it is said of Christ (Matthew 12:8) that he is 'Lord even of the sabbath day'?

A. By no means; the very contrary will follow, namely, that such a seventh part of weekly time, as is now observed, is moral, because he who is the Lord of the Sabbath has appointed it to be so; and, consequently, has power to order the work of it for his own service.

Q. 42. Is it any argument against the morality of the Sabbath, that it 'was made for man, and not man for the Sabbath'?

A. No; but rather an argument for it. The meaning doubtless is that resting on the Sabbath was appointed for man's good, that it might be a means to a further and better end, even the true sanctification of it in the exercise of the duties of piety and mercy required on the day.

Shorter Catechism question 59

Which day of the seven hath God appointed to be the weekly Sabbath?

From the beginning of the world to the resurrection of Christ, God appointed the seventh day of the week to be the weekly Sabbath; and the first day of the week ever since, to continue to the end of the world, which is the Christian Sabbath.[65]

Q. 1. When did God appoint the seventh day of the week to be the weekly Sabbath?

A. 'From the beginning of the world' (Genesis 2:2-3).

Q. 2. Why is it said to be 'from the beginning of the world' when it was not done till after man was created on the sixth day?

A. Because the world, as to its perfection of parts, did not properly begin till the creation was completely finished, which was not till man was made, who was to have dominion over all the earth.[66]

Q. 3. How long was this seventh or last day of the week appointed to be the weekly Sabbath?

---

65 Genesis 2:2-3. And on the seventh day God ended his work which he had made; and *he rested on the seventh day from all his work* which he had made. And God *blessed the seventh day, and sanctified it*: because that in it he had rested from all his work which God created and made.

1 Corinthians 16:1-2. Now concerning the collection for the saints, as I have given order to the churches of Galatia, *even so do ye. Upon the first day of the week* let every one of you lay by him in store, as God hath prospered him, that there be no gatherings when I come.

Acts 20:7. *And upon the first day of the week, when the disciples came together to break bread,* Paul preached unto them, ready to depart on the morrow; and continued his speech until midnight.

66 Genesis 1:26. And God said, Let us make man in our image, after our likeness: and let them have dominion over the fish of the sea, and over the fowl of the air, and over the cattle, and over all the earth, and over every creeping thing that creepeth upon the earth.

A. 'To the resurrection of Christ' (Matthew 28:1).

Q. 4. Which day of the week did God appoint for the Sabbath 'ever since' that time?

A. 'The first day of the week' (Acts 20:7).

Q. 5. For how long time is the first day of the week appointed to be the weekly Sabbath?

A. 'To the end of the world'.

Q. 6. How are we sure that it is appointed 'to continue to the end of the world'?

A. Because the canon of Scripture is concluded, and therefore no new revelations and institutions are to be expected.[67]

Q. 7. Why is the first day of the week called 'the Christian Sabbath'?

A. Because it was instituted by Christ, and uniformly observed by Christians ever since his resurrection.

Q. 8. Are not all divine institutions observed in virtue of some moral precept?

A. Yes; otherwise the law of the Lord would not be perfect, as it is declared to be.[68]

Q. 9. In virtue of what moral precept has the first day of the week been observed by Christians?

A. In virtue of the fourth commandment; even as the means of worship,

---

67 Revelation 22:18-19. For I testify unto every man that heareth the words of the prophecy of this book, If any man shall add unto these things, God shall add unto him the plagues that are written in this book: and if any man shall take away from the words of the book of this prophecy, God shall take away his part out of the book of life, and out of the holy city, and from the things which are written in this book.

68 Psalm 19:7. The law of the LORD is perfect, converting the soul: the testimony of the LORD is sure, making wise the simple.

instituted under the New Testament, have been observed in virtue of the second.

Q. 10. How can the first day of the week be observed in virtue of the fourth commandment, when it is not in it particularly mentioned?

A. The morality of the Sabbath does not lie in observing the seventh day in order from the creation, but in observing such a seventh day as is determined and appointed by God; which may be either the first or last of the seven days, as he shall see meet.

Q. 11. Under what name or designation is the Christian Sabbath foretold in the Old Testament?

A. Under the name of the 'eighth day' (Ezekiel 43:27): 'And when these days are expired, it shall be that upon the eighth, and so forward, the priests shall make your burnt offerings upon the altar, and your peace offerings: and I will accept you, saith the Lord.'

Q. 12. Why called the eighth day?

A. Because the first day of the week now, is the eighth in order from the creation.

Q. 13. What is the efficient cause of the change of the Sabbath?

A. The sovereign will and pleasure of him who is 'Lord of the sabbath' (Mark 2:28).

Q. 14. What is the moving cause of this change?

A. The resurrection of Christ from the dead, which was 'early on the first day of the week' (Mark 16:9).

Q. 15. Why is the day of Christ's resurrection appointed to be the Sabbath?

A. Because his resurrection was a demonstrative evidence that he had completely finished the glorious work of redemption;[69] and therefore it was his resting day (Hebrews 4:10): 'He that is entered into his rest, he also hath ceased from his own works, as God did from his.'

Q. 16. Why might not the day of Christ's incarnation or the day of his passion, have been consecrated to be our Sabbath Day?

A. Because they were both of them days of Christ's labour and sorrow, which he had to go through before he came to his rest.[70] In his incarnation and birth he entered upon his work.[71] In his passion [sufferings] he was under the sorest part of his labour, even the exquisite and unspeakable agonies of his soul.[72]

Q. 17. Why might not the day of his ascension be made the Sabbath, as well as the day of his resurrection?

A. Because on the day of his ascension he entered only into his *place* of rest, the third heavens; whereas he had entered before into his *state* of rest on the day of his resurrection; and the place is but a circumstance, when compared with the state.

Q. 18. Why did God change his day of rest?

A. Because his rest in the work of creation was marred and spoiled by man's sin;[73] whereas his rest in the work of redemption, entered into at the resurrection of Christ, is that in which he will have eternal and

---

69   Romans 1:4. And declared to be the Son of God with power, according to the spirit of holiness, by the resurrection from the dead.

70   Luke 24:26. Ought not Christ to have suffered these things, and to enter into his glory?

71   Galatians 4:4-5. But when the fulness of the time was come, God sent forth his Son, made of a woman, made under the law, to redeem them that were under the law, that we might receive the adoption of sons.

72   Matthew 26:38. Then saith he unto them, My soul is exceeding sorrowful, even unto death: tarry ye here, and watch with me.

73   Genesis 6:6. And it repented the LORD that he had made man on the earth, and it grieved him at his heart.

71

unchangeable pleasure.[74] Besides, redemption is a far greater and more excellent work than even that of creation.

Q. 19. How may the change of the Sabbath from the last to the first day of the week be evinced from Scripture?

A. If our Lord Jesus, after his resurrection, met ordinarily with his disciples on the first day of the week; if, after his ascension, he poured out his Spirit in an extraordinary manner on that day; if, by the example and practice of the apostles and primitive Christians, recorded in the New Testament, the first day of the week was honoured above any other for the public exercises of God's worship; if, by apostolic precept, the observance of this day, rather than any other, was enjoined for Sabbath services; and if this day is peculiarly dignified with the title of 'the Lord's Day', then it must undoubtedly be the Christian Sabbath by divine institution.

Q. 20. How does it appear that our Lord, after his resurrection, met ordinarily with his disciples on the first day of the week?

A. From two instances of it, expressly recorded;[75] where it is affirmed that he met with them on the evening of the same day on which he arose from the dead, being the first day of the week, and that Thomas was not with them when Jesus came.[76] Likewise, on that same day eight days [a week later], he appeared to them again, when they 'were within, and Thomas was with them' (John 20:26). From whence it would seem that

---

74 John 17:23. I in them, and thou in me, that they may be made perfect in one; and that the world may know that thou hast sent me, and hast loved them, as thou hast loved me.

75 John 20:19, 26. Then the same day at evening, being the first day of the week, when the doors were shut where the disciples were assembled for fear of the Jews, came Jesus and stood in the midst, and saith unto them, Peace be unto you. And after eight days again his disciples were within, and Thomas with them: then came Jesus, the doors being shut, and stood in the midst, and said, Peace be unto you.

76 John 20:24. But Thomas, one of the twelve, called Didymus, was not with them when Jesus came.

he met with them ordinarily on that day, during his forty days' abode on the earth after his resurrection.

Q. 21. How is it evident that Christ, after his ascension, poured out his Spirit in an extraordinary manner on this day?
A. From Acts 2:1-5: 'And when the day of Pentecost was fully come, they were all with one accord, in one place. And suddenly there came a sound from heaven. [...] And they were all filled with the Holy Ghost', etc.

Q. 22. What was the day of Pentecost?
A. It was the fiftieth day after the passover, when the 'new meat offering' was brought unto the Lord.[77]

Q. 23. How do you prove that this was the first day of the week?
A. From Leviticus 23:16; where it is said, that the morrow after the seventh Sabbath is the fiftieth day (or Pentecost). And it is certain that the morrow after the Jewish Sabbath must be the first day of the week.

Q. 24. How does it appear, from the example and practice of the apostles and primitive Christians, that the first day of the week was honoured above any other for the public exercise of God's worship?
A. From Acts 20:7: 'And on the first day of the week, when the disciples came together to break bread, Paul preached unto them,' where it is obvious that the disciples met ordinarily upon the first day of the week to hear the Word and celebrate the sacrament of the supper; for it is not said, the apostle called them, but that they 'came together to break bread', and Paul on that occasion 'preached unto them'.

---

77 Numbers 28:26. Also in the day of the firstfruits, when ye bring a new meat offering unto the LORD, after your weeks be out, ye shall have an holy convocation; ye shall do no servile work.

Q. 25. How may it be proved from the context, that the disciples met ordinarily for the public exercises of God's worship, on the first day of the week?

A. That they did so may be proved from this, that 'Paul abode with them seven days' as is evident from verse 6, and yet upon none of the seven did they meet for communicating, or breaking of bread, but on the first day of the week only; which plainly says that they held it for the Christian Sabbath, and not the seventh or last day, which is not even mentioned.

Q. 26. But do we not read (Acts 13:14) that Paul preached in a synagogue on the Sabbath Day, which certainly behoved to be the Jewish Sabbath or last day of the week?

A. He only preached occasionally on the Jewish Sabbath, as the fittest time, when the Jews were assembled together, to dispense Gospel truth among them; but did not honour this day as a stated time for public worship.

Q. 27. What apostolic precept is there for the observance of the first day of the week, rather than any other, for Sabbath services?

A. It is in 1 Corinthians 16:1-2: 'Now, concerning the collection for the saints, as I have given order to the churches of Galatia, even so do ye. Upon the first day of the week, let every one of you lay by him in store, as God hath prospered him.'

Q. 28. What is the argument from this text to prove an apostolic precept for observing the first day of the week as the Christian Sabbath?

A. It may run thus: That if collections for the poor are expressly commanded to be made on the first day of the week, it plainly follows that Christians must meet together on that day, for this and other Sabbath services.

Q. 29. But may not this be a temporary precept, binding for a time upon the church of Corinth only?

A. As the words of the text expressly affirm that it was binding also upon the churches of Galatia, so the apostle directs his epistle not to the church of Corinth only, but to 'all that in every place call upon the name of Jesus Christ' (Galatians 1:2); and consequently it must be binding upon all the churches to the end of the world.

Q. 30. In what place of the New Testament is there mention made of a day dignified with the title of 'the Lord's Day'?

A. In Revelation 1:10: 'I was in the Spirit,' says John, 'on the Lord's day'.

Q. 31. How may it be proved that what is here called the Lord's Day is the first day of the week?

A. By these two arguments: That no other day of the week but the first that can justly be called the Lord's Day; and that the first day of the week is so called in virtue of Christ's sanctifying it, above any other day, for his own honour and service.

Q. 32. Why can no other day of the week, but the first, be justly called the Lord's Day?

A. Because there is no action or work of Christ (save healing on the Sabbath) mentioned or recorded as done upon any one day of the week by another, except that of his resurrection, which is unanimously affirmed by the evangelists, to be on the first day of the week.

Q. 33. How does it appear that the first day of the week is called the Lord's Day, in virtue of his sanctifying it for his own honour and service?

A. As the seventh day Sabbath was called the Sabbath of the Lord, because instituted by him as God-Creator, so the first day of the week is called the Lord's Day, because instituted by him as God-Redeemer; or, as the sacrament of bread and wine is called the Lord's Table and the

Lord's Supper[78] because it is an ordinance of his institution, so the first day of the week is called the Lord's Day for the very same reason.

Q. 34. Would the apostles have observed and recommended the first day of the week for the Christian Sabbath, if they had not been particularly instructed in this by Christ himself?

A. No, surely; for after his passion [suffering and death] he spoke of the things pertaining to the kingdom of God,[79] among which the change of the Sabbath from the last to the first day of the week was none of the least; and it is certain that the apostles delivered nothing to the churches, as a rule of faith or practice, but what they received of the Lord.[80]

---

78   1 Corinthians 10:21. Ye cannot drink the cup of the Lord, and the cup of devils: ye cannot be partakers of the Lord's table, and of the table of devils.
1 Corinthians 11:20. When ye come together therefore into one place, this is not to eat the Lord's supper.

79   Acts 1:3. To whom also he shewed himself alive after his passion by many infallible proofs, being seen of them forty days, and speaking of the things pertaining to the kingdom of God.

80   1 Corinthians 11:23. For I have received of the Lord that which also I delivered unto you.

Shorter Catechism question 60

How is the Sabbath to be sanctified?

The Sabbath is to be sanctified by a holy resting on that day,[81] even from such worldly employments and recreations as are lawful on other days;[82] and spending the whole time in the public and private exercises of God's worship,[83] except so much as is to be taken up in the works of necessity and mercy.[84]

---

81   Exodus 20:8, 10. *Remember the sabbath day, to keep it holy.* But the seventh day is the *sabbath of the* LORD *thy God: in it thou shalt not do any work,* thou, nor thy son, etc.
Exodus 16:25-28. And Moses said, Eat that to day; for to day is a sabbath unto the LORD: to day ye shall not find it in the field. Six days ye shall gather it; but on the seventh day, which is the sabbath, in it there shall be none. And it came to pass, that there went out some of the people on the seventh day for to gather, and they found none. And the LORD said unto Moses, How long refuse ye to keep my commandments and my laws?

82   Nehemiah 13:15-22. In those days saw I in Judah some *treading wine presses on the sabbath, and bringing in sheaves, and lading asses; as also wine, grapes, and figs, and all manner of burdens,* which they brought into Jerusalem on the sabbath day: and *I testified against them in the day wherein they sold victuals.* There dwelt men of Tyre also therein, *which brought fish, and all manner of ware, and sold on the sabbath* unto the children of Judah, and in Jerusalem. *Then I contended with the nobles of Judah, and said unto them, What evil thing is this that ye do, and profane the sabbath day?* Did not your fathers thus, and did not our God bring all this evil upon us, and upon this city? yet ye bring more wrath upon Israel by profaning the sabbath. And it came to pass, that when the gates of Jerusalem began to be dark before the sabbath, I commanded that the gates should be shut, and charged that they should not be opened till after the sabbath: and some of my servants set I at the gates, that there should no burden be brought in on the sabbath day. So the merchants and sellers of all kind of ware lodged without Jerusalem once or twice. Then I testified against them, and said unto them, *Why lodge ye about the wall?* If ye do so again, I will lay hands on you. From that time forth *came they no more on the sabbath.* And I commanded the Levites that they should cleanse themselves, and that they should come and keep the gates, to sanctify the sabbath day. Remember me, O my God, concerning this also, and spare me according to the greatness of thy mercy.

83   Luke 4:16. And he came to Nazareth, where he had been brought up: and, as his custom was, he went into the synagogue *on the sabbath day, and stood up for to read.*

Q. 1. In what sense is the Sabbath to be sanctified?

A. As it is dedicated by God for man's sake and use, that he may keep it holy to God.

Q. 2. In what manner should he keep it holy to God?

A. By 'a holy resting' and by 'holy exercises'.

Q. 3. What should we rest from on the Sabbath?

A. 'Even from such worldly employments and recreations as are lawful on other days' or, which is the same thing, from all servile work.[85]

Q. 4. What is it that makes a work servile?

A. If it is done for our worldly gain, profit and livelihood; or if, by

---

Acts 20:7. *And upon the first day of the week, when the disciples came together to break bread,* Paul preached unto them, ready to depart on the morrow; and continued his speech until midnight. Psalm 92 (title). A Psalm or Song for the sabbath day.

Isaiah 66:23. And it shall come to pass, that from one new moon to another, and *from one sabbath to another, shall all flesh come to worship before me,* saith the LORD.

84 Matthew 12:1-31 (verses 1-2, 12 cited). At that time Jesus went on the sabbath day through the corn; and his disciples were an hungred, and began to pluck the ears of corn, and to eat. But when the Pharisees, etc. [...] *It is lawful to do well on the sabbath days.*

85 Nehemiah 13:15-23. In those days saw I in Judah some treading wine presses on the sabbath, and bringing in sheaves, and lading asses; as also wine, grapes, and figs, and all manner of burdens, which they brought into Jerusalem on the sabbath day: and I testified against them in the day wherein they sold victuals. There dwelt men of Tyre also therein, which brought fish, and all manner of ware, and sold on the sabbath unto the children of Judah, and in Jerusalem. Then I contended with the nobles of Judah, and said unto them, What evil thing is this that ye do, and profane the sabbath day? Did not your fathers thus, and did not our God bring all this evil upon us, and upon this city? yet ye bring more wrath upon Israel by profaning the sabbath. And it came to pass, that when the gates of Jerusalem began to be dark before the sabbath, I commanded that the gates should be shut, and charged that they should not be opened till after the sabbath: and some of my servants set I at the gates, that there should no burden be brought in on the sabbath day. So the merchants and sellers of all kind of ware lodged without Jerusalem once or twice. Then I testified against them, and said unto them, Why lodge ye about the wall? If ye do so again, I will lay hands on you. From that time forth came they no more on the sabbath. And I commanded the Levites that they should cleanse themselves, and that they should come and keep the gates, to sanctify the sabbath day. Remember me, O my God, concerning this also, and spare me according to the greatness of thy mercy.

prudent management, it might have been done the week before; or, if it be of such a kind as may be delayed till after the Sabbath.[86]

Q. 5. Why does God enjoin rest on the Sabbath so peremptorily, and particularly in the time of ploughing and harvest?
A. Because in these seasons men are most keenly set upon their labour, and may be in the greatest hazard of grudging the time of the Sabbath for rest.

Q. 6. If the weather is unseasonable through the week, do not reaping and ingathering in that case become works of necessity on the Sabbath?
A. By no means; because any unseasonableness of the weather that may happen, being common and general, proceeds only from the course of God's ordinary providence, which we ought not to distrust, in regard of his promise that 'while the earth remaineth, seed-time and harvest ... shall not cease' (Genesis 8:22).

Q. 7. If a field of corn is in hazard of being carried away by the unexpected inundation of a river, is it lawful to endeavour the preservation of them upon the Sabbath?
A. Yes; because the dispensation is extraordinary, the case not common nor general, and the damage likewise, in an ordinary way, is irrecoverable.

Q. 8. Are Christians, under the New Testament, obliged to as strict an abstinence from worldly labour as the Jews were under the Old?
A. Yes, surely; for moral duties being of unchangeable obligation, Christians must be bound to as strict a performance of them now, as the Jews were then.[87]

---

86   Exodus 34:21. Six days thou shalt work, but on the seventh day thou shalt rest: in earing time [ploughing time or seed time] and in harvest thou shalt rest.

Q. 9. Were not the Jews prohibited to dress meat on the Sabbath?[88]
A. They were prohibited such servile work as was requisite in preparing manna for food, such as the grinding of it in mills, beating it in mortars and baking it in pans;[89] but not all dressing of meat for the comfortable nourishment of their bodies, any more than we.

Q. 10. How does it appear that they were allowed to dress meat on the Sabbath for the comfortable nourishment of their bodies?
A. From our Lord's being present at a meal on the Sabbath Day, to which there were several guests bidden, and consequently meat behoved to be prepared and dressed for their entertainment.[90]

Q. 11. Were not the Jews forbidden to kindle fire in their habitations upon the Sabbath Day?[91]
A. Yes; for any servile work, though it were even making materials for the tabernacle (which is the work spoken of through the following part of that chapter), but they were not forbidden to kindle fires for works of necessity or mercy, any more than Christians are.

---

87   Psalm 19:9. The fear of the LORD is clean, enduring for ever: the judgments of the LORD are true and righteous altogether.

88   Exodus 16:23. And he said unto them, This is that which the Lord hath said, To morrow is the rest of the holy sabbath unto the Lord: bake that which ye will bake to day, and seethe that ye will seethe; and that which remaineth over lay up for you to be kept until the morning.

89   Numbers 11:8. And the people went about, and gathered it, and ground it in mills, or beat it in a mortar, and baked it in pans, and made cakes of it: and the taste of it was as the taste of fresh oil.

90   Luke 14:1-6. And it came to pass, as he went into the house of one of the chief Pharisees to eat bread on the sabbath day, that they watched him. And, behold, there was a certain man before him which had the dropsy. And Jesus answering spake unto the lawyers and Pharisees, saying, Is it lawful to heal on the sabbath day? And they held their peace. And he took him, and healed him, and let him go; and answered them, saying, Which of you shall have an ass or an ox fallen into a pit, and will not straightway pull him out on the sabbath day? And they could not answer him again to these things.

91   Exodus 35:3. Ye shall kindle no fire throughout your habitations upon the sabbath day.

Q. 12. Were they not ordered to abide every man in his place, and not to go out of his place on the seventh day?[92]

A. The prohibition only respects their going abroad about the unnecessary and servile work of gathering manna upon the Sabbath; otherwise they were allowed to go out about works of necessity and mercy, and it appears from Acts 1:12 that they were allowed to travel 'a sabbath day's journey'.

Q. 13. What was 'a sabbath day's journey'?

A. Whatever was the tradition of the Pharisees about it, it appears to have been the distance of their respective dwellings from the place where they ordinarily attended public ordinances.[93]

Q. 14. Are we not to rest on the Lord's Day from lawful recreations as well as from lawful worldly employments?

A. Yes; because we are expressly required, on this holy day, to abstain from doing our own ways, finding our own pleasure and speaking our own words.[94]

Q. 15. What are these recreations that are lawful on other days?

A. Innocent pastimes, visiting friends, walking in the fields, talking of the news or common affairs, and the like.

---

92   Exodus 16:29. See, for that the LORD hath given you the sabbath, therefore he giveth you on the sixth day the bread of two days; abide ye every man in his place, let no man go out of his place on the seventh day.

93   2 Kings 4:23. And he said, Wherefore wilt thou go to him to day? it is neither new moon, nor sabbath. And she said, It shall be well.

94   Isaiah 58:13-14. If thou turn away thy foot from the sabbath, from doing thy pleasure on my holy day; and call the sabbath a delight, the holy of the LORD, honourable; and shalt honour him, not doing thine own ways, nor finding thine own pleasure, nor speaking thine own words: then shalt thou delight thyself in the LORD; and I will cause thee to ride upon the high places of the earth, and feed thee with the heritage of Jacob thy father: for the mouth of the LORD hath spoken it.

Q. 16. Why are these recreations unlawful on the Lord's Day?

A. Because they tend to divert the mind from the duties of the Sabbath as much as, if not more than, worldly employments.

Q. 17. Is not the Sabbath a festival or feast day, and consequently may not our conversation on it be cheerful and diverting?

A. It is indeed properly a feast day, but of a spiritual, not of a carnal, nature; we may refresh our bodies moderately, but not sumptuously; and our conversation ought to turn wholly upon spiritual and heavenly subjects, or such as have that tendency, after the example of our Lord.[95]

Q. 18. What should be the principal end of our six days' labour?

A. That it be so managed as in no way to discompose or unfit us for a holy resting on the Sabbath or meeting with God on his own day.

Q. 19. What is 'a holy resting'?

A. Not only an abstaining from our own work or labour, but an entering by faith (in the use of appointed means) into the presence and enjoyment of God in Christ as the only rest of our souls;[96] that having no work of our own to mind or do, we may be wholly taken up with the works of God.

Q. 20. Why called a *holy* resting?

A. Because we should rest from worldly labour in order to be employed in the holy exercises which the Lord requires on this day; otherwise, as to bare cessation, our cattle rest from outward labour as well as we.

---

95 Luke 14:1, 2, 5. And it came to pass, as he went into the house of one of the chief Pharisees to eat bread on the sabbath day, that they watched him. And, behold, there was a certain man before him which had the dropsy. […] And answered them, saying, Which of you shall have an ass or an ox fallen into a pit, and will not straightway pull him out on the sabbath day?

96 Hebrews 4:3. For we which have believed do enter into rest, as he said, As I have sworn in my wrath, if they shall enter into my rest: although the works were finished from the foundation of the world.

Q. 21. What are the holy exercises in which we ought to be employed on the Lord's Day?

A. 'In the public and private exercises of God's worship'.

Q. 22. What are the public exercises of God's worship in which we should be employed?

A. Hearing the word preached,[97] joining in public prayers and praises,[98] and partaking of the sacraments.[99]

Q. 23. What are included under the private exercises of God's worship?

A. Family and secret duties.

Q. 24. What are the duties incumbent on us in a family capacity on the Lord's Day?

A. Family worship and family catechising, together with Christian conference, as there is occasion (Leviticus 23:3): 'It is the Sabbath of the Lord in all your *dwellings*' or private families, and therefore God is to he worshipped in them on that day.

Q. 25. What is family worship?

A. It is the daily joining of all that are united in a domestic relation, or who are dwelling together in the same house and family, in singing God's praises,[100] reading his word[101] and praying to him.[102]

---

97   Romans 10:17. So then faith cometh by hearing, and hearing by the word of God.

98   Luke 24:53. And [they] were continually in the temple, praising and blessing God.

99   Acts 20:7. And upon the first *day* of the week, when the disciples came together to break bread, Paul preached unto them, ready to depart on the morrow; and continued his speech until midnight.

100   Acts 2:46-47. And they, continuing daily with one accord in the temple, and breaking bread from house to house, did eat their meat with gladness and singleness of heart, praising God, and having favour with all the people. And the Lord added to the church daily such as should be saved.

Q. 26. How do you prove family worship to be a duty daily incumbent upon those who have families?

A. From Scripture precept and from Scripture example.

Q. 27. How is family worship evinced from Scripture precept?

A. Besides this commandment enjoining every master of a family to sanctify the Sabbath within his gates (that is, to worship God in his family), there are also other Scriptures inculcating the same thing by necessary consequence, such as Ephesians 6:18: 'Praying always, with all prayer and supplication'; 1 Timothy 2:8: 'I will therefore that men pray every where.' If with all prayer, then surely with family prayer; if every where, then certainly in our families.

Q. 28. What are the examples of family worship recorded in Scripture for our imitation?

A. Among others, there are the examples of Abraham,[103] of Joshua,[104] of David,[105] of Cornelius[106] and, to crown all, the example of our blessed Lord, whom we find singing psalms[107] and praying with his disciples, who were his family.[108]

---

101 Deuteronomy 6:7. And thou shalt teach them diligently unto thy children, and shalt talk of them when thou sittest in thine house, and when thou walkest by the way, and when thou liest down, and when thou risest up.

102 Jeremiah 10:25. Pour out thy fury upon the heathen that know thee not, and upon the families that call not on thy name: for they have eaten up Jacob, and devoured him, and consumed him, and have made his habitation desolate.

103 Genesis 18:19. For I know him, that he will command his children and his household after him, and they shall keep the way of the LORD, to do justice and judgment; that the LORD may bring upon Abraham that which he hath spoken of him.

104 Joshua 24:15. As for me and my house, we will serve the LORD.

105 2 Samuel 6:20. Then David returned to bless his household.

106 Acts 10:1-2. There was a certain man in Caesarea called Cornelius, a centurion of the band called the Italian band, a devout man, and one that feared God with all his house, which gave much alms to the people, and prayed to God alway.

107 Matthew 26:30. And when they had sung an hymn, they went out into the mount of Olives.

108 Luke 9:18. And it came to pass, as he was alone praying, his disciples were with him.

Q. 29. What should be the subject matter of family catechising?

A. What they have been hearing through the day, together with the principles of our religion as laid out in the Shorter Catechism, with the helps that are published on the same, which masters of families ought to use for their assistance in this work.

Q. 30. What are the proper seasons of Christian conference on the Sabbath?

A. At meals, and in the interval of duties; our speech should be always, but especially on the Lord's Day, 'seasoned with salt' (Colossians 4:6).

Q. 31. What are the secret duties in which we ought to be exercised on the Lord's Day?

A. Secret prayer, reading the Scriptures and other soul-edifying books, meditation upon divine subjects, and self-examination.

Q. 32. With what frame and disposition of soul should we go about the public and private exercises of God's worship?

A. With a spiritual frame and disposition (Revelation 1:10): 'I was in the Spirit on the Lord's day'.

Q. 33. What is it to be 'in the Spirit on the Lord's day'?

A. It is not only to have the actual inhabitation of the Spirit, which is the privilege of believers every day,[109] but to have the influences and operations of the Spirit more liberally let out[110] and his graces in a more lively exercise than at other times.[111]

---

109 Ezekiel 36:27. And I will put my spirit within you, and cause you to walk in my statutes, and ye shall keep my judgments, and do them.

110 Luke 4:30-32. But he passing through the midst of them went his way, and came down to Capernaum, a city of Galilee, and taught them on the sabbath days. And they were astonished at his doctrine: for his word was with power.

111 Acts 2:41. Then they that gladly received his word were baptized: and the same day there were added unto them about three thousand souls.

Q. 34. What moral argument do we have from the ceremonial law for offering a greater plenty of spiritual sacrifices to God on the Sabbath, than upon other days?

A. The daily sacrifice, or continual burnt offering, was to be doubled on the Sabbath,[112] intimating that they were bound to double their devotions on that day, which was consecrated to God to be spent in his service.

Q. 35. How much of the Sabbath is to be spent in the public and private exercises of God's worship?

A. The *whole* of it, from the ordinary time of rising on other days to the ordinary time of going to rest, 'except so much as is to be taken up in the works of necessity and mercy'.

Q. 36. What is to be understood by 'works of necessity'?

A. Such as could not be foreseen or provided against the day before, nor delayed till the day after the Sabbath.

Q. 37. What instances may be given of such works of necessity on the Lord's Day?

A. Fleeing from and defending ourselves against an enemy, quenching of fire accidentally or wilfully kindled, standing by the helm or working a ship at sea (provided they do not weigh anchor or hoist sail from harbours or firths on the Lord's day), and the like.

Q. 38. What are the 'works of mercy' which may be done on the Sabbath?

---

112 Numbers 28:8-10. And the other lamb shalt thou offer at even: as the meat offering of the morning, and as the drink offering thereof, thou shalt offer it, a sacrifice made by fire, of a sweet savour unto the LORD. And on the sabbath day two lambs of the first year without spot, and two tenth deals of flour for a meat offering, mingled with oil, and the drink offering thereof: this is the burnt offering of every sabbath, beside the continual burnt offering, and his drink offering.

A. The moderate refreshment of our bodies,[113] visiting the sick, preparing and administering remedies to them,[114] feeding our cattle[115] and pre-serving their lives if in danger,[116] and making collections for the poor.[117]

Q. 39. What cautions are requisite about works of necessity and mercy?

A. That these works be real, and not pretended; that we spend as little time about them as possible and that we endeavour to attain a holy frame of spirit while about them.

Q. 40. How does it appear that works of necessity and mercy are lawful on the Lord's Day?

A. Because, though God rested from his work of creation on the seventh day, yet he did not rest on it from preserving what he had made.

Q. 41. Why is the charge of keeping the Sabbath more especially directed to governors of families and other superiors?[118]

A. 'Because they are bound not only to keep it themselves, but to see that it be observed by all those that are under their charge; and because they are prone ofttimes to hinder them by employments of their own.'[119]

Q. 42. Ought not magistrates to punish those who are guilty of the

---

113　Luke 6:1. And it came to pass on the second sabbath after the first, that he went through the corn fields; and his disciples plucked the ears of corn, and did eat, rubbing them in their hands.

114　Luke 13:16. And ought not this woman, being a daughter of Abraham, whom Satan hath bound, lo, these eighteen years, be loosed from this bond on the sabbath day?

115　Luke 13:15. The Lord then answered him, and said, Thou hypocrite, doth not each one of you on the sabbath loose his ox or his ass from the stall, and lead him away to watering?

116　Luke 14:5. And answered them, saying, Which of you shall have an ass or an ox fallen into a pit, and will not straightway pull him out on the sabbath day?

117　1 Corinthians 16:2. Upon the first day of the week let every one of you lay by him in store, as God hath prospered him, that there be no gatherings when I come.

118　The question is replicated from the Larger Catechism, question 118.

119　The answer is a quotation from the answer to question 118 in the Larger Catechism.

open and presumptuous breach of the Sabbath?

A. Undoubtedly they should; and they have the example of Nehemiah for a precedent, worthy of their imitation in this matter.[120]

Q. 43. What is the most effectual way for the civil magistrate to suppress Sabbath profanation?

A. To be impartial in the execution of the laws against Sabbath breaking, especially upon those who are of a more eminent rank and station, because they ought to be exemplary to others (Nehemiah 13:17): 'Then I contended with the nobles of Judah; and said unto them, What evil thing is this that ye do, and profane the sabbath day?'

Q. 44. Why is the word 'remember' set in the beginning of the fourth commandment?[121]

A. Partly because we are very ready to forget it, and partly because in keeping it we are helped better to keep all the rest of the commandments.[122]

---

120 Nehemiah 13:21. Then I testified against them, and said unto them, Why lodge ye about the wall? if ye do so again, I will lay hands on you. From that time forth came they no more on the sabbath.

121 The question is replicated from the Larger Catechism, question 121.

122 The answer paraphrases part of the answer to question 121 in the Larger Catechism.

Shorter Catechism question 61

What is forbidden in the fourth commandment?

The fourth commandment forbiddeth the omission or careless performance of the duties required,[123] and the profaning the day by idleness,[124] or
doing that which is in itself sinful,[125] or by unnecessary thoughts, words,
or works, about our worldly employments and recreations.[126]

---

123 Ezekiel 22:26. *Her priests have violated my law*, and have profaned mine holy things: they have put
no difference between the holy and profane, neither have they shewed difference between the
unclean and the clean, and *have hid their eyes from my sabbaths*, and I am profaned among them.
Amos 8:5. Saying, When will the new moon be gone, that we may sell corn? and *the sabbath, that
we may set forth wheat*, making the ephah small, and the shekel great, and falsifying the balances
by deceit?
Malachi 1:13. Ye said also, Behold, *what a weariness is it!* and ye have snuffed at it, saith the
LORD of hosts; and ye brought that which was torn, and the lame, and the sick; thus ye
brought an offering: should I accept this of your hand? saith the LORD.

124 Acts 20:7, 9. And upon the first day of the week, when the disciples came together to break
bread, Paul preached unto them, ready to depart on the morrow; and continued his speech
until midnight. And there sat in a window a certain young man named Eutychus, being *fallen
into a deep sleep*: and as Paul was long preaching, he sunk down with sleep, and fell down from
the third loft, and was taken up dead.

125 Ezekiel 23:38. Moreover this they have done unto me: they have defiled my sanctuary in the
same day, and *have profaned my sabbaths*.

126 Jeremiah 17:24-26. And it shall come to pass, if ye diligently hearken unto me, saith the LORD,
to bring in no burden through the gates of this city *on the sabbath day*, but hallow the sabbath day, *to
do no work therein*; then shall there enter into the gates of this city kings and princes sitting upon
the throne of David, riding in chariots and on horses, they, and their princes, the men of
Judah, and the inhabitants of Jerusalem: and this city shall remain for ever. And they shall
come from the cities of Judah, and from the places about Jerusalem, and from the land of
Benjamin, and from the plain, and from the mountains, and from the south, bringing burnt
offerings, and sacrifices, and meat offerings, and incense, and bringing sacrifices of praise, unto
the house of the LORD.
Isaiah 58:13. If thou turn away thy foot from the sabbath, *from doing thy pleasure on my holy day*;
and call the sabbath a delight, the holy of the LORD, honourable; and shalt honour him, *not
doing thine own ways, nor finding thine own pleasure, nor speaking thine own words*.

Q. 1. How are the sins ranked that are forbidden in this command-ment?
A. They are ranked into sins of omission and sins of commission.

Q. 2. What are the sins of *omission* here forbidden?
A. Both the total neglect of the duties required and the neglect of the careful performance of these, when essayed.

Q. 3. Of what is the total neglect of the duties required on the Sabbath an evidence?
A. It is a plain evidence of the neglect of all religious duties through the week, and consequently an evidence of atheism, profaneness and apostasy.

Q. 4. When are persons guilty of the 'careless performance of the duties required' on the Sabbath?
A. When they go about them in a partial, formal and lifeless way.[127]

Q. 5. What is it to go about duties in a partial way?
A. It is to perform some of them and omit others equally necessary, such as attending the public, and neglecting the private, exercises of God's worship, or the contrary.

Q. 6. What is formality in duty?
A. It is the bare outward performance of it, without regarding the manner in which it ought to be done, or the vital principle from whence it should flow.[128]

Q. 7. What are the ordinary causes of the dead and lifeless performance of religious duties?

---

127 Matthew 15:8. This people draweth nigh unto me with their mouth, and honoureth me with their lips; but their heart is far from me.

128 2 Timothy 3:5. Having a form of godliness, but denying the power thereof: from such turn away.

WHAT IS FORBIDDEN IN THE FOURTH COMMANDMENT?

A. Wandering thoughts, weariness and drowsiness are among none of the least.

Q. 8. What is the best antidote against wandering thoughts?
A. Faith in exercise; for this will fix the attention to what we are presently engaged in, whether hearing, praying or praising.[129]

Q. 9. Whence arises weariness in duty?
A. From the natural bias of the heart and affections to worldly things, rather than religious exercises (Amos 8:5): 'When will the new moon be gone, that we may sell corn? and the sabbath, that we may set forth wheat?'

Q. 10. What is the evil of drowsiness, particularly in hearing the word, or joining in prayer and praise?
A. If it be voluntary and customary, it is a manifest contempt of the Word and presence of the great God, and paying less regard to him than we even do to our fellow creatures.

Q. 11. What are the sins of *commission* forbidden in this commandment?
A. 'The profaning the day by idleness or doing that which is in itself sinful, or by unnecessary thoughts, words, or works, about our worldly employments and recreations'.

Q. 12. What is the 'idleness' here prohibited?
A. It is a loitering away the Sabbath, in a slothful, indolent and inactive manner, without any real benefit or advantage either to soul or body.[130]

Q. 13. Why is there a prohibition of 'doing that which is in itself sinful' on the Lord's Day, when it is unlawful on every other day?
A. Because whatever the sinful action be, there is a greater aggravation of

---

129 Psalm 57:7. My heart is fixed, O God, my heart is fixed: I will sing and give praise.
130 Matthew 20:3. And he went out about the third hour, and saw others standing idle in the marketplace.

guilt in committing it on the Sabbath, which ought to be kept holy to God, than upon any other day.[131]

Q. 14. What are these 'thoughts, words, or works', that are here called 'unnecessary'?

A. They are such as are 'about our worldly employments and recreations'; or, they are all such thoughts, words or works as are not inevitably used about the works of necessity and mercy, which are lawful on this day.

Q. 15. Why is the day said to be profaned by the sins here forbidden?

A. Because these sins are each of them the reverse of that holiness which should shine in all our duties, public and private, on the Lord's Day.[132]

---

131 Jeremiah 17:27. But if ye will not hearken unto me to hallow the sabbath day, and not to bear a burden, even entering in at the gates of Jerusalem on the sabbath day; then will I kindle a fire in the gates thereof, and it shall devour the palaces of Jerusalem, and it shall not be quenched.

132 Isaiah 58:13-14. If thou turn away thy foot from the sabbath, from doing thy pleasure on my holy day; and call the sabbath a delight, the holy of the LORD, honourable; and shalt honour him, not doing thine own ways, nor finding thine own pleasure, nor speaking thine own words: then shalt thou delight thyself in the LORD; and I will cause thee to ride upon the high places of the earth, and feed thee with the heritage of Jacob thy father: for the mouth of the LORD hath spoken it.

Shorter Catechism question 62

What are the reasons annexed to the fourth commandment?
The reasons annexed to the fourth commandment are, God's allowing us six days of the week for our own employments,[133] his challenging a special propriety in the seventh, his own example, and his blessing the sabbath day.[134]

Q. 1. How many reasons are there annexed to this commandment?
A. Four; which are more than to any of the rest.

Q. 2. Why are more reasons annexed to this command than to any of the rest?
A. Because of the proneness of men to break it, and likewise that the violation of it may be rendered the more inexcusable.

Q. 3. Which is the first reason?
A. It is 'God's allowing us six days of the week for our own employments' in these words, 'Six days shalt thou labour and do all thy work'.

Q. 4. In what lies the strength of this reason?
A. It lies in this, that it would be most highly unreasonable and ungrateful to grudge a seventh part of our time in the more immediate service and worship of God, when he has been so liberal as to allow us six parts of it for our own secular and worldly affairs.

Q. 5. What similar instance of ingratitude may be given for the illustration of this?

---

133 Exodus 20:9. *Six days shalt thou labour,* and do all thy work.
134 Exodus 20:11. For in six days the LORD made heaven and earth, the sea, and all that in them is, and rested the seventh day: wherefore the LORD *blessed the sabbath day,* and hallowed it.

A. The sin of our first parents in refusing to abstain from one tree, when they were allowed the free use of all the rest of the garden.[135]

Q. 6. Is working six days in our own employment a precept properly belonging to this commandment?

A. No; it is properly a branch of the eighth commandment, but it is brought in here incidentally, to enforce the sacred observance of a seventh day, when God has been so bountiful as to allow us six for our own occasions.

Q. 7. Which is the second reason annexed to this commandment?

A. It is 'his challenging a special propriety in the seventh' in these words, 'But the seventh day is the sabbath of the Lord thy God'.

Q. 8. What is the force of this reason?

A. The force of it is this: as that gracious God, who makes a grant of himself to us in the covenant of promise, claims this day as his own, so it is our greatest privilege or happiness to have access to and communion with him on it.[136]

Q. 9. In what lies the privilege or happiness of communion with God on his own day?

A. In having a foretaste in grace here of what shall be more fully enjoyed in glory hereafter.[137]

---

135 Genesis 3:2, 3, 6. And the woman said unto the serpent, We may eat of the fruit of the trees of the garden: but of the fruit of the tree which is in the midst of the garden, God hath said, Ye shall not eat of it, neither shall ye touch it, lest ye die. And when the woman saw that the tree was good for food, and that it was pleasant to the eyes, and a tree to be desired to make one wise, she took of the fruit thereof, and did eat, and gave also unto her husband with her; and he did eat.

136 Isaiah 58:14. Then shalt thou delight thyself in the LORD; and I will cause thee to ride upon the high places of the earth, and feed thee with the heritage of Jacob thy father: for the mouth of the LORD hath spoken it.

137 1 Corinthians 13:12. For now we see through a glass, darkly; but then face to face: now I know in part; but then shall I know even as also I am known.

Q. 10. Which is the third reason?

A. It is 'his own example' in these words, 'For in six days the Lord made heaven and earth, the sea, and all that in them is, and rested the seventh day.'

Q. 11. Could not God have made heaven and earth, the sea, and all that in them is, in less time than the space of six days?

A. No doubt; he could have made all things, in the same beauty and perfection in which ever they appeared, in an instant of time, if he had pleased.

Q. 12. Why then did he take six days?

A. To fix the morality of six days for worldly labour and of a seventh for holy rest; and both these by his own example.

Q. 13. But does not the example of God's resting the seventh day oblige us still to observe the seventh day, in order from the creation, as a Sabbath?

A. No; because, though moral examples bind always to the kind of action, yet not always to every particular circumstance of it.

Q. 14. What is the kind of action to which God's example binds us?

A. It is to observe one day in seven for holy resting, either the last or first, as he shall appoint.

Q. 15. How can God's example of resting on the seventh day be an argument for our resting on the first?

A. Though the observance of a particular day in seven be *mutable*, yet the duty of observing a seventh part of weekly time is *moral*, both by God's precept and example.

Q. 16. Which is the fourth reason annexed to this commandment?

A. It is 'his blessing the sabbath day' in these words, 'Wherefore, the Lord blessed the sabbath day, and hallowed it.'

Q. 17. In what sense may the Sabbath be said to be blessed?

A. Not only by God's consecrating the day itself to a holy use, but by his blessing it to the true observers of it, and by his blessing them in it.

Q. 18. How does God bless the Sabbath to the true observers of it?

A. By ordering it so in his providence, that the religious observance of the Sabbath shall be no detriment to, but rather a furtherance of, their lawful employments through the week; even as the profanation of it draws a train of all miseries and woes after it.[138]

Q. 19. How does he bless them in it, or upon it?

A. By making it the happy season of a more plenteous communication of all spiritual blessings to them.[139]

Q. 20. What does the illative particle [a word denoting an inference] 'wherefore' teach us?

A. That God's resting on the Sabbath was the great reason of his setting it apart to be a day of holy rest to us, that on it we might contemplate the works of God, both of creation and redemption.

---

138 Nehemiah 13:18. Did not your fathers thus, and did not our God bring all this evil upon us, and upon this city? yet ye bring more wrath upon Israel by profaning the sabbath.

139 Isaiah 58:14. Then shalt thou delight thyself in the LORD; and I will cause thee to ride upon the high places of the earth, and feed thee with the heritage of Jacob thy father: for the mouth of the LORD hath spoken it.

Part 3

The Fourth Commandment

Dr John Kennedy, Dingwall

Lecture by Rev Dr John Kennedy

Delivered at Dingwall
16th September 1883

The purpose of this lecture is to direct attention to the divine authority and perpetual obligation of the fourth commandment, to consider what it requires and, under its light, to inquire how the Sabbath law is regarded in our land and to inquire to what extent the Sabbath is sanctified by ourselves.

The divine authority and perpetual obligation of the fourth commandment

This commandment is the fourth of the statutes composing the moral law which, because of the number of commandments that are found in it, is usually called the Decalogue [the Ten Words]. It is the last of those written on the first table of the law, and which declare the form in which love to God should be expressed in obedience.

There could be no doubt in the mind of any who compassed Mount Sinai that the law promulgated there issued from Jehovah, for 'the sight of the glory of the Lord was like devouring fire on the top of the mount in the eyes of the children of Israel'. Amidst blackness, and darkness, and tempest shone the flame of the devouring fire. The awful blast of the trumpet thundered, and a 'voice of words' came forth from the fire. The mountain quaked, and all the earth around it was shaken. It was no wonder that the people were overwhelmed with terror, when even Moses said, 'I exceedingly fear and quake.' Who amidst the assembly, before such a scene as Sinai then presented, hearing the awful thunder and 'the voice of words', and feeling the earth quaking beneath them, could doubt that they were in the presence of Jehovah, and that from him came the law which was delivered to them by Moses on two tables of stone? Thus came from God to Israel the fourth commandment, with all the other words of the Decalogue.

The words of the law, spoken by Jehovah's mouth, were engraved by his finger on tables of stone. Surely this suffices to indicate that this summary of duty was intended by him to be perpetual. The Ten Commandments alone were thus written by God. Not thus did he write the rules prescribing the typical service of Israel, for the binding obligation of these was intended to be but temporary, and must in due season pass away. But the Decalogue was intended to be perpetual, and there was therefore a divine engraving of it on stone.

But it may be said – yea, it has often been said – that the observance of the Sabbath was made binding, by the law given forth on Sinai, only on the children of Israel. Not so, for the terms of the commandment bring its obligation to bear on 'the stranger', and godly Nehemiah enforced the observance of it on Gentiles as well as on Jews. True, the revelation of the moral law was given exclusively to Israel in the wilderness. They, and they only, heard 'the voice of words' coming from the awful glory of 'the mount that might be touched, and that burned with fire'. But what was then given to them on tables of stone was placed in their custody for all mankind. It was not because they were God's peculiar people that they were under obligation to obey the moral law, but because, like all other rational beings on the face of the earth, they were bound to keep all the commandments of God. It was not the *obligation* but the *revelation* of the Decalogue that was peculiar to Israel.

And as to the fourth commandment, it requires only what was required from the beginning. The Sabbath was instituted by God in Eden, and was there both enjoined and observed. The first day of human history was a Sabbath, and those who feared the Lord in the pre-Mosaic times doubtless remembered the Sabbath Day to keep it holy.

Christ distinctly tells us 'that the sabbath was made for man', not for the Jew only. There was a Sabbath long before there was a Jew. Man, everywhere and at all times, needs it; and men of all nations are enjoined to observe it, and all who despise it act not only unwisely but wickedly.

And what reason can be given for representing the Sabbath as a Jewish institution? Why should the fourth commandment, rather than any other, be represented as but of limited and temporary obligation? There is certainly nothing in the form of it to give it a peculiarity on account of which it should be so regarded and treated. The tribute which it demands for God must surely always be due to him; and what reason can be given why the memorial of his rest after the work of creation should not be continued? And if the giving of a Sabbath to man be a boon, what but a change, affecting the goodness of God, could account for its being withdrawn? The fourth commandment is 'good' as well as 'just and holy', and while the goodness of God is unchanged, it cannot cease to require the keeping holy of the Sabbath. I could imagine some reason for saying that the fifth commandment has a Jewish cast, because the promise subjoined to it refers to the land which the Lord their God had given to Israel. This, it might be said, is surely spoken only to the Jews, because of the evident reference to the land of Canaan which, according to the promise of the Lord, was given exclusively to them. But the question as to its perpetual obligation is conclusively settled in the New Testament, for Paul, writing to the Ephesians, asserts the binding force of that commandment; and calling it 'the first commandment with promise', insists on the perpetual connection between obedience to it and the promise which is subjoined to the precept. 'It *is*', not it *was*, he tells us, 'the first commandment with promise'.

The claim of the fourth commandment rests on *moral*, not on *positive* grounds. It demands for God what is due to him in his unchanging supremacy, majesty and glory. Can we conceive of rational beings – under the reign of one who is 'infinite, eternal, and unchangeable, in his being' and in all his attributes – not under obligation to separate themselves at certain seasons from all employment besides, in order to do homage in worship to the Most High? Why, even to an earthly sovereign – a fellow creature – direct homage is due when the sovereign chooses to require it. The time prescribed for this must be remembered, and used for the appointed purpose. And is it to be imagined that men who, because of their lot on earth, are necessarily employed about mere secular things, can be free from an obligation to detach themselves 'from their worldly employments and recreations' in order to render homage to 'the high and lofty One who inhabiteth eternity, and whose name is Holy'? It is inconceivable how any mind, influenced by right views of the greatness of Jehovah and not forgetful of our entire dependence on his goodness, could approach to think of the obligation of the fourth commandment not being *moral, and therefore universal and perpetual.*

And if the homage demanded is due to God, he has the right to determine when and how that homage is to be rendered. Our Queen demands a right to fix when a reception takes place, and how those who are to be presented shall appear in her presence. And surely this right must be conceded to God. He has exercised this right, which rests on his supremacy as Jehovah. He has determined that a seventh of each week shall be devoted, so far as possible, in consistency with meeting the claims of necessity and mercy, exclusively to his worship – the ground of that allotment being given us in his own example as Creator. Surely, then, not only is the demand for a Sabbath one resting on unchanging moral grounds, but the portion of time to be observed as a Sabbath is unalterably fixed.

There are thus two fixed points, which can admit of no change, in the requirements of the fourth commandment – the one is that there be a Sabbath devoted exclusively to the service of God, and the other is that one day in each week shall be so devoted. Neither of these is at all affected by the change implied in making the *first* day of the week the Christian Sabbath instead of the seventh. This change was made by him who had a right to do so, and who in view of it declared himself to be 'Lord of the Sabbath'. How could he who appointed the Sabbath at the beginning, and who promulgated the Sabbath law from Sinai, be expected to exercise his lordship over it by setting it aside? It was in view of its continuing to be under his administration, as exalted to the throne, the Son of Man proclaimed himself its Lord. If he discountenanced a Pharisaic observance of that day, and was so careful, both by precept and example, to rebuke those who substituted a punctilious formality for the true spiritual observance of the Sabbath, is that a reason for supposing that the Sabbath law was to be abrogated? Nay, is not his care regarding its being rightly observed a reason why we should be assured of the Lord's regard for it, and that, under his reign, the fourth commandment would be of binding force till time shall be no more?

Was Christ not entitled to effect the change? He was the Creator, in memorial of whose rest the seventh day was appointed to be the Sabbath. In his view all his creation work was good, and he rested, in complacency [pleasure], his eye on all that he had finished. A memorial of that rest we might expect him to give, and it was given to man, and the Lord made it man's interest as well as his duty to observe it. And if he who acted thus in connection with his finished work, as Creator, performed a work still greater – a work in which was manifested, as in no other work besides, the glory of all his name, and to which all creation and providence were subordinated – how could we but expect a memorial of his entering into his rest when that work was finished?

Instead of the change of day being inconsistent with the perpetual obligation of the fourth commandment, it is that perpetual obligation which makes the change imperative. Just because the seventh day was the Sabbath of old, as a memorial of the rest of God after finishing his work as Creator, the first day must be so now, as a memorial of his rest after finishing the work of redemption.

The antecedent action of God demands the change. If he owed it to himself to make the one day a memorial of his rest after creation, all the more does he owe it to himself, to set apart the other as a memorial of a rest still more glorious. For it is he who appointed the Sabbath of old who, in his resurrection from the dead, began to enter into his rest after the work of redemption was finished. The very instinct of the church would crave the giving of a memorial of that day. And it was given, and that too in such a way as, while not removing the memorial of the Lord's rest after creation, gave to his rest, after redemption, the place which was due to it because of the exceeding greatness of the work which preceded it. Sufficient, in the tribute rendered to God, as a concession to the greatness of creation work, is the retaining of the proportion of time to be observed as a Sabbath holy to the Lord. What kind of mind must be that of a man who imagines that, because of the fuller manifestation of the divine glory and the glorious commendation of divine love through Christ crucified, a tribute which Jehovah was wont to claim is no longer exacted and should no longer be rendered?

And it is sufficiently proved that the day was changed by divine authority from the seventh to the first of the week. The example of Christ and the practice of the apostles, as recorded in the New Testament, sufficiently prove this to be the case. What can be more authoritative, as a directory to the Church, than the example of the Church's Head and the practice and writing of his inspired apostles? And we have his example in his coming once and again to his disciples after his resurrection to countenance their meeting for worship on the first day of the week. And the practice of the pre-Ascension days was continued thereafter by the apostles; and Paul, writing to the Corinthians, mentions 'the first day of the week' as the day of gathering together for worship, as well as of 'collection for the saints'.

The very lack of an express enactment making the change imperative is an eloquent tribute to the authoritative action of God bearing on the Sabbath in the days of old, and to the value and authority of Christ's example. There was no need of a re-enactment of the Sabbath law, for he who enacted it at first sufficiently declared that he intended it to be perpetual, and with him 'is no variableness, neither shadow of turning'. And if he countenanced the change of the Sabbath from the seventh day to the first, what can be more authoritative than his example as a rule of duty?

Why then, it may be asked, is there such a desire to get rid of the perpetual obligation of the fourth commandment, as requiring the observance of the Christian Sabbath? Certainly not because there is any reasonable ground for supposing that the fourth commandment has been removed from its place in the Decalogue, nor because the change of day is not only *allowable* and *authoritative*, but *morally necessary*. This desire to be rid of a Sabbath law arises from its being peculiarly testing. It requires the actual surrender of one day in seven to be a holy Sabbath to the Lord. The refusal of such a surrender is a palpable thing, of which even a very slumbering conscience must take note and regard as sin, and which must be apparent to the eyes of onlookers. It is in order to escape from the strictures of conscience and to secure boldness to sin before

105

men that there are such efforts to prove that the Sabbath law is repealed. This is the secret spring of the whole anti-Sabbatarian movement. Ungodly men desire to be free to do as they list on the day of the Lord, and they think they can secure this by an impotent attack on the perpetual authority of the fourth commandment. They, forsooth, who are but worms of the dust, are to overthrow the arrangements of the Most High, and over his shattered law are to reach an emancipation from being under responsibility to God! This is their daring behest, and they imagine that by flippant objections, which but betrays their ignorance and their profanity, they can secure what they desire and thus obtain a triumph, which entitles them to be mockers of the saints of God.

What is required in the fourth commandment?

Looked at in the light of this commandment, the Sabbath is a day which the Lord has blessed and hallowed. He has set it apart from every other day by so blessing it that it becomes a blessing to all who rightly observe it. No one who has not proved it by a spiritual observance of it can know what a blessing it is, or has a right to pronounce any judgment regarding it. But none ever honestly proved it who did not experience it to be a blessing from the Lord. And the Lord has hallowed it. He has done so in setting it apart from other days as specially his own – as a day to be devoted to his worship.

In accordance with this dedication of it by God, the Sabbath is required to be *remembered* and *kept holy*. In order to *remem'ber* it one must think of it as a day which the Lord has blessed. He must be conscious of his need of such a blessing as the Sabbath was intended to be, and be anxious to enjoy it, as well as have the divine authority of the commandment bearing on his conscience. And he must *keep it holy*. He must act becomingly towards it as a day which the Lord has hallowed. He must heartily call it a delight, as it is 'holy to the Lord and honourable', and seek grace to preserve him from devoting any portion of it to any work which accords not with the design of God in hallowing it. The worship of God, private and public, is the work to which the hours of one entire day in seven is to be devoted, except in so far as (in connection with our lot on earth and the course of providence) we are called to engage in 'works of necessity and mercy'. From love to God, expressed in regarding his Sabbath as a delight, and in seeking the enjoyment of his gracious presence and fellowship on that day, we must be quite willing to withdraw ourselves from 'all such employments and recreations as are lawful on other days' and heartily devote ourselves to the service of God.

According to the terms of the commandment, not only is the individual bound to keep the Sabbath holy, but each one having influence is bound to exert that influence in endeavouring to secure the observance of the Sabbath by those who are under him. The parent and master are thus bound to use their influence. They are specified in the words of the commandment; but the same obligation rests on all who hold a position of influence to a greater or less extent over their fellow-men. All employers of labour, all judges and magistrates, all employed in connection with the executive government of the nation, the legislature, the Sovereign, are all under obligation, imposed by divine authority, to use all their power in securing that the Sabbath of the Lord is hallowed.

How is the Sabbath observed in Scotland?

It would be far more pleasant to consider the past than the present of our country's relation to the law of the Sabbath. The time was when the Sabbath law was so observed in Scotland that she was marked, because of this, as singular among all lands; and while her practice was a joy to all lovers of the law of God it won for her the honour of being reproached by all who were enemies of truth and godliness. To some extent that reproach has not been quite removed. Scotland has not yet become such that her distinctive Sabbatarianism is so blotted out by the increase of practical ungodliness that she can no longer favourably compare with other nations. But it is sad to think of how far her departure from 'the good way' of Sabbath-keeping has already gone.

What a contrast a Scottish Sabbath now presents to that of earlier times – to that even of the generation which has just passed away! Think of our railway trains rushing over all parts of the country with their thousands of passengers, disturbing the Sabbath quiet and tempting so many to forget that there is a 'God in the earth who judgeth righteously'. Think of so many open shops along the streets of our cities on the day of rest, which is the day of God, and receiving such support as tempts ungodly men to extend the traffic [trade]. Think of the increasing crowds of those to whom the Sabbath has become a day of amusements, who never think of entering a place of worship and who, by their conduct, prove that vice is the ally of ungodliness. Think of how even those, who are not prepared utterly to abandon the public worship of God, are beginning to act as if an enforced partial attendance in the courts of God's house earns for them a right to do what they please on what remains of the Sabbath. Think, too, of the easy tolerance of such practices already so apparent in the unfaithful supineness both of the Church and of the State while all this desecration of the Sabbath is in progress. Think of all these things – and what a contrast the Scottish Sabbath of today presents to that of times gone by! And what unspeakably greater contrast is the present observance of the day of the Lord to 'what is required in the fourth commandment'!

To this sad result, unfaithful discipline, on the part of the churches, has greatly contributed. On a communion Sabbath members of the church are allowed to come to the table of the Lord, who, on all other Sabbaths of the year, care not even to appear to have any regard to the requirements of the law of God. And not a few will leave the table of the Lord to rush to amusements in the evening. And this is endured! And a church, pledged to preserve the purity of the house and the sanctity of the day of the Lord, endures it! In this respect what a contrast church discipline presents to that of other times! There may have been an extremeness in the mode of exercising discipline in earlier times, but it expressed zeal for the honour of God's law and for the purity of his house. An opposite extreme has now been reached, which expresses no more creditable feeling than indifference as to the claims of God, and as to the welfare of precious souls.

And the action of the State, in relation to the Sabbath law, combines with that of the churches to hasten Scotland's departure from 'the old paths'. All legislation in defence of the rest and sanctity of the Sabbath is refused, and almost all forms and measures of Sabbath desecration are tolerated. Of this we, in this county, have had a notable example [see Foreword]. A wanton and flagrant desecration of the Sabbath, by railway officials and their servants, occurred. And not only was there no interference on the part of the executive to put down the excuseless traffic [trade], but all exertions were put forth, by those who should be 'a terror to evil-doers', to protect it. And arrangements were made for shooting down the men whose only crime was a pronounced expression of zeal in behalf of the Sabbath law of heaven and of Scotland, in the event of their persisting in their opposition to what they regarded as defiant transgression of the fourth commandment. The civil magistrate thus became a praise to evil-doers, and a terror to them that do well. Woe to Scotland when such are those by whom the law is administered! But what was done in connection with the Sabbath desecration at Strome, is, in spirit, in accordance with the rule of all the action – or inaction – bearing on the Sabbath, of the executive throughout our country. An instance so flagrant as that to which I have referred, of those in authority condoning the conduct of men who, in their eager thirst for gain, scruple not to trample the law of God under foot, cannot yet be quoted. But the spirit which appeared then in a form so exceptionally pronounced, seems to be that by which our rulers are animated. And in due time, if the Lord does not graciously interfere, the people of our country will learn tamely to submit to any action in which it may be expressed.

And the leading newspapers of the country add their influence to all that tends to remove the authority of the fourth commandment from the consciences of the people. One of these - the most widely circulated, and whose name [*The Scotsman*] claims for it the position of being the representative of Scottish opinion – the organ of infidel liberalism, is never more earnest and envenomed in its paragraphs than when it utters its ignorant sneers at all Sabbath-keeping, and pours out its abuse on those by whom the Sabbath law is defended. On some minds this must tell. The reiteration of its sceptical mockery of what is Scriptural must, to some extent, affect the feeling of those who are unacquainted with the Word of God, and care not seriously to consider any subject to which their attention may be directed. And the number of such may be counted by thousands. There are a few whom its attacks on all that was once deemed sacred in Scotland cannot affect, except with indignation and sorrow – indignation because of how what is sacred is boldly profaned, and sorrow because of how views are propagated which tend to the temporal, as surely as to the spiritual, deterioration of the people. This would seem to be the *aim*, as well as the natural *result* of the work, of *The Scotsman*; for, while it pleads for a wholesale Sabbath profanation, it strenuously supports the oppressor against the poor crofters of the Highlands. If any zeal is exhibited by them on behalf of the Sabbath, the poor Highlanders are abused as criminals, but when their grievances are being inquired into, all its kindliness is reserved for those by whom these were imposed. Remorseless is the cruelty of those who would insist on a continuance of the oppression that offers to our people, as the only alternative, starvation in their fatherland or emigration to the further ends of the earth, in order that a pampered aristocracy may have their desired amusement. And this is the outcome of the infidel liberalism of our times! But more cruel still it is to endeavour to induce our working classes to utterly abandon the 'godliness' which has 'the promise of this life' as well as of 'that which is to come'.

What infatuation the conduct of our aristocracy and of our rulers indicates, when by the example of the former, and the guilty indifferentism of the latter, the country people of this nation are induced to treat with contempt the claims of the fourth commandment! The next commandment which follows is that which secures for them a right to be respected and obeyed, and in no measure can anyone be truly disposed to yield to them their due, who have ceased to pay respect to the claims of God. By refusing to follow and enforce the Sabbath law, they are doing what they can to secure a revolution in our native land. From the Sabbath-breaking masses will come the great danger of the future; for a people, trained to disregard the demand of God, that his Sabbath shall be hallowed, and whose grievances remain unredressed, shall soon cease to have any respect for those to whom, according to the law of God, they owe dutiful submission.

How is the Sabbath observed among us and by ourselves?

This is a question which each one of us is bound to consider, for on each of us rests an obligation to do what the fourth commandment requires. You cannot by any possibility get rid of this obligation. And the obligation is divinely imposed. Some may imagine they are in a position up to which the claim of the Sabbath law does not rise – that it is something to which the vulgar alone are called to have respect. And the poor, amidst the pinching straits of their lot, may think that to them Sabbath-keeping is impossible, and is therefore not required of them. Others still, found among the highest and among the lowest in rank may imagine that, by the aid of men of advanced opinions, they have reached a conclusion which entirely disposes of the Sabbath law and relieves them of all responsibility in connection with it. And, besides all these, there are many who think that any seemly measure of outward respect for the Sabbath is a full discharge of all that is dutiful; while there are some whose official work is such that they cannot refrain from seeming to respect it. But to each one of all these classes the question is addressed, and to it an answer must be given, if not earlier, most certainly at the bar of the great court of assize at the last day.

How are you affected towards the Sabbath in your heart?

Do you rejoice in prospect of it, not because its rest from toil is craved by your wearied body and by your mind from worrying business, but because it is a day 'holy to the Lord, and honourable'? Are you on that account really disposed to call it 'a delight'? Does the prospect of enjoying communion with the Lord, and of enjoying 'peace' in 'his ways' give you gladness? Does your desire for this induce you to pray to God in prospect of the Sabbath for his presence and his blessing?

When the Sabbath comes, how are you employed in your closet?

Is there any true spiritual worship there? Do not imagine that there can be any genuine worship in public if there be no true worship in secret. If you seek God at all you will seek him in your closet. True godliness is not a bit of gaudy patchwork for the eyes of men to observe; it is a spiritual living with God in secret prayer, in which there are wrestlings for his blessing, sighings under the hiding of his face, gladness in the hope of his favour, joy in meditation on his glory and his love as revealed through Jesus Christ, and glimpses by the eye of faith of the coming glory, and foretastes of it such as cause fervent longings for the time when that glory shall be reached. What do you know of such exercises as these in your closet on the day of God?

112

How is it as to family worship on Sabbath?

Is there an altar to God in your household? Do you enjoy the service of compassing it? Do you in that work seek the face and strength of the Lord? O, how sad it is to think of families that never take part in any such service! And sad, too, is the case of all heads of households who regard family worship as an uninteresting routine which, if they dared, they would altogether omit!

How is it as to household duties on the Sabbath?

Is unnecessary work avoided? Are such arrangements made and observed, as will admit of as many members of the household as possible attending in the place of public worship? What is done by parents in the religious instruction of their children? This is a duty binding on every parent, and it must fare ill with every community in which this is neglected. The home is the nursery of the church, and nothing else can supply the place of parental instruction of the young. The tendency in these days is to delegate this work to the teachers in our Sabbath schools. Many parents feel as if the opportunity of sending their children to be instructed elsewhere had relieved them of all responsibility in connection with their being taught at home. But this is an utter mistake, and is an evil, in connection with our Sabbath school system, which ought to be carefully guarded against. True, there are parents who are both indisposed to be dutiful to their children, and quite incapable of rightly instructing them. Other instruction than that which their parents can give them is required by the children of such as these. But let that be given to them in their own homes, by office-bearers of the church and Christian friends to whom such work would be a labour of love. The parents might thus learn while their children were being taught, and might, by the blessing of God, be stirred up to, and fitted for, the discharge of their duty as instructors of their children.

113

Our Sabbath school system, in the measure in which it tends to separate parents and children, cannot but have an injurious effect. It causes a separation of them beyond what is immediate. The Sabbath school is becoming the children's church, as distinguished from the parents' church, and it is becoming a rarer thing than once it was to see the parents and children together in the house of God. In some places already the extreme has been reached of the entire absence of children from the house of God when the Gospel is preached, and the proposal has been made (and partially acted on) of having a quite separate children's church. And with their work in the Sabbath school, which is naturally looked on as their only public worship on Sabbath, how apt are the children to associate what they have been accustomed to in their ordinary gatherings during the week! And how prejudicially this must tell on their respect for the day of the Lord! Sabbath-keeping cannot therefore be expected to be the fruit of large gatherings of children in Sabbath schools. And the habit of confining the religious teaching of the young to the Sabbath school tends on the one hand, to make the parents utterly regardless as to their duty, and on the other, to make the rising generation indifferent as to stated attendance in the house of God.

I am afraid that neither Sabbath observance, nor regular Sabbath attendance in the place of worship, shall be found to be the fruit of our Sabbath schools. But they seem to be indispensable, and the church's work should, in connection with them, be to do what is possible in order to secure that the children shall be taught at home by parents competent to instruct them, and that the children of undutiful and incompetent parents be taught in circulating little groups in the several households to which they belong.

What is your Sabbath reading?

There never was a time when so many books for Sabbath reading issued from the press. 'Sunday' – the heathenish name for the Lord's Day – is

114

put on the title page of some of these, and this is almost all that is Sabbatic about them. Tales and illustrations are mingled with singularly light religious pap, in order to gratify a taste that says of the Sabbath, 'When will it be gone?' and to which searching the Scriptures is a weariness. There is nothing that ought to take the place of the prayerful study of the Word of God; and let your other reading be confined to works which have been approved by the church and blessed by the Lord.

What is your public worship?

How are you affected towards it? Are you truly conscious of your need of grace to prepare you for engaging in it in a spiritual frame of mind? Do you feel your need of receiving instruction, and are you more ready to hear than to offer the sacrifice of fools? Know you what it is to feel sad in his house when the Lord withholds his gracious presence? Has 'a day in his courts' been to you, in your experience, 'better than a thousand'? Or has your coming to the house of God been to you a mere matter of habit – a mere lifeless formality?

These are questions which demand the serious attention of each one of you all. Dare not to make so light of the claims of God, as not to care what answers you can honestly give.

Warnings against bad examples and misrepresentations

I desire, before I close, to warn you, and especially the young, against *examples* and *misrepresentations* from which you may be in danger.

Warnings against bad examples

I would warn you against the example of Sabbath walking. Such an example is presented to you, though certainly not by any who, in their practice, are entitled to your respect. Still, the very habit of seeing others doing what, in your conscience, you cannot approve, may have an evil influence, and as the observed transgression of the law of God increases,

115

in that measure is the volume of the current which endangers your steadfastness. I know few more excuseless things than this Sabbath walking. If the plea of health is used to justify it, how can men expect *that* to benefit their health which they dare not ask the Lord to bless? And if they can only plead that they do it for recreation, because they feel the Sabbath to be dull, how can they dare to act in a way which so plainly indicates their dislike of the day and of the Word of God? And surely what ought chiefly to be sought on the Sabbath is what would be an eternal benefit to the soul. And if so, what possible advantage, in order to the acquisition of this, can be found in the society or surroundings of those who go forth on his day, openly to exhibit their contempt of the Lord. This way of profaning the Sabbath has often been the beginning of a career of crime. Beware of it, my young friends.

Beware, too, of following the example of those who cannot dispense with having their letters and newspapers on Sabbath. No one can listen to the plea of necessity in favour of sending for letters to the Post Office on Sabbath, or of requiring that these be delivered to them. Forsooth, *they* cannot dispense with them, though in London, the busiest and wealthiest city in the world, no letters are received on Sabbath. If the exigencies of business might be pled anywhere in behalf of a Sabbath delivery of letters, surely it is there. And in our paltry villages, petty businessmen must have their letters, to whatever extent this may involve a profanation of the day of rest! And some of our gentry, as if anxious that all should be informed of their contempt for what is sacred, will send their mounted couriers to the country offices, to which they laboured to secure that despatches should be carried. They need not be so careful to exhibit their disregard for the law of God, for the information, given in this pronounced form, was already in possession of the public. Men of graceless hearts and benighted minds were not suspected of being able to endure to lack the contents of letters and newspapers, the only kind of reading which they can appreciate, and by which they can be pleased. If they are determined to call the Sabbath a weariness, let them do so to their own eternal ruin; but by no law is a right given to them, by an ostentation of their ungodliness, to grieve the hearts of those who think that 'the law of God is holy, and just, and good'.

Warnings against misrepresentations

Do not be cheated with infidel objections to careful Sabbath-keeping, however smartly and sneeringly these may be uttered. As the tide of declension is moving on, an impression is produced in the hearts of those who are adrift that all things which they are leaving behind them are but relics of darker times. Adherence to what is antiquated is all that is implied, they say, in the conservatism that cleaves to 'the old paths' and 'the good way' in which our fathers walked. It is characteristic of young men that they do not like to appear to be behind the age. They must be abreast of the intelligence of a century so enlightened as this is. They must cast away the old clothes of traditionalism, and must learn to sneer at the days and ways that are gone, that they may be like those who assume to be the leaders of thought – the advanced guard of the army of progress. They must neither think nor speak like the men of earlier and, therefore, more benighted times! To minds of this cast, access is easy to the idea of the Sabbath and of Sabbath-keeping being things of the past, and therefore not to be respected. But, my young friends, be not led away by this affectation of progress with its contempt for what is past. There never was a time when in science there was more utterly baseless speculation, and in which more structures of lies were reared within the religious sphere, than now.

There never was an age of more hasty thinking and of more hazy utterance than the present in all things affecting what is divine and spiritual. But God is unchanging. On that grand truth firmly plant your foot in faith. The law of God is unchanging. That truth is another strong foothold. On these be 'steadfast and unmovable' in the midst of all present unsettlement of thought and practice, and all the influence which may be brought to bear upon you will not suffice to cause you to regard Sabbath-keeping as a thing which any generation should leave behind it.

Careful Sabbath-keeping will be represented to you as a gloomy thing. And by whom? By those who always carefully refrained from trying what sort of thing it was. If you are, like them, not a lover of the Sabbath yourself, you are quite sure to be a coward before a scaring bugbear such as this. You will find Sabbath-keeping gloomy, not because it is so, but because you dislike to attempt it. Forsooth, there should not be a Sabbath because there are many sinful men who do not like it! God must adapt his laws to the liking of his enemies! If you would wish to know whether Sabbath-keeping is gloomy work, ask those who have tried what it is. They will tell you that it is 'a delight'. They would not exchange one moment's gladness, such as they have enjoyed on the Lord's Day in his fellowship and service, for all that the world could bestow of its dissipating pleasures. It is just in the measure in which they are not unreserved in their devotion of the day to God that these, who alone are competent to pronounce a decision, find the Sabbath to be gloomy. The Sabbath requiring to borrow from the world in order that it may not be a gloomy thing to observe it! Can men talk more insanely when they speak thus? A man is happier because he forsakes 'the fountain of living waters' and betakes himself to 'broken cisterns'? Men are gloomy, whose joy is to be enlightened with the glory of God and touched by the love of God, as compared with those who have no more to make them glad than what can be won in a service whose wages is death?

Let neither the enemies of God not your own evil heart give you your estimate of the Sabbath. Take that only from the Word of God, and seek from God a heart that will love what he commands and move you to walk as he commands – and then I am certain that you will cease to regard the Sabbath as a weariness, or the keeping of it as a thing of gloom. Then will you find as much of gladness in Sabbath-keeping as will enable you to disregard the sneers of those who would fain mock you back from the ways of righteousness. And you will find as much of gladness in Sabbath-keeping as will enable you to despise the pleasures by which they would tempt you to desecrate the day of the Lord.

Appendix

The Sabbath Day

Westminster Confession of Faith
with Scripture proofs

Confession of Faith – Chapter 23, section 7

As it is the law of nature, that, in general, a due proportion of time be set apart for the worship of God; so, in his Word, by a positive, moral, and perpetual commandment, binding all men, in all ages, he hath particularly appointed one day in seven, for a Sabbath, to be kept holy unto him:[140] which, from the beginning of the world to the resurrection of Christ, was the last day of the week; and, from the resurrection of Christ, was changed into the first day of the week,[141] which, in Scripture, is called the

---

140 Exodus 20:8, 10-11. *Remember the sabbath day, to keep it holy.* [...] *But the seventh day is the sabbath of the LORD thy God: in it thou shalt not do any work,* thou, nor thy son, nor thy daughter, thy manservant, nor thy maidservant, nor thy cattle, nor thy stranger that is within thy gates: for in six days the LORD made heaven and earth, the sea, and all that in them is, and *rested the seventh day: wherefore the LORD blessed the sabbath day, and hallowed it.*
Isaiah 56: 2, 4, 6-7. Blessed is the man that doeth this, and the son of man that layeth hold on it; *that keepeth the sabbath from polluting it,* and keepeth his hand from doing any evil. ... For thus saith the LORD unto the eunuchs that *keep my sabbaths,* and choose the things that please me, and take hold of my covenant; ... Also the sons of the stranger, that *join themselves to the LORD, to serve him,* and to love the name of the LORD, to be his servants, every one that keepeth the sabbath from polluting it, and taketh hold of my covenant; even *them will I bring to my holy mountain, and make them joyful in my house of prayer:* their burnt offerings and their sacrifices shall be accepted upon mine altar; for *mine house shall be called an house of prayer for all people.*
141 Genesis 2:2-3. And on the seventh day God ended his work which he had made; and *he rested on the seventh day* from all his work which he had made. And God *blessed the seventh day, and sanctified it:* because that in it he had rested from all his work which God created and made.
1 Corinthians 16:1-2. Now concerning the collection for the saints, as I have given order to the churches of Galatia, even so do ye. *Upon the first day of the week* let every one of you lay by him in store, as God hath prospered him, that there be no gatherings when I come.
Acts 20:7. And *upon the first day of the week,* when the disciples came together to break bread, Paul preached unto them, ready to depart on the morrow; and continued his speech until midnight.

Lord's Day,[142] and is to be continued to the end of the world, as the Christian Sabbath.[143]

---

142 Revelation 1:10. I was in the Spirit *on the Lord's day*, and heard behind me a great voice, as of a trumpet.

143 Exodus 20:8, 10. *Remember the sabbath day, to keep it holy. But the seventh day is the sabbath of the LORD thy God: in it thou shalt not do any work*, thou, nor thy son, nor thy daughter, thy manservant, nor thy maidservant, nor thy cattle, nor thy stranger that is within thy gates.
With Matthew 5:17-18. *Think not that I am come to destroy the law, or the prophets: I am not come to destroy, but to fulfil.* For verily I say unto you, Till heaven and earth pass, *one jot or one tittle shall in no wise pass from the law, till all be fulfilled.*

Confession of Faith – Chapter 23, section 8

This Sabbath is then kept holy unto the Lord, when men, after a due preparing of their hearts, and ordering of their common affairs beforehand, do not only observe an holy rest, from their own works, words, and thoughts about their worldly employments, and recreations,[144] but

---

144 Exodus 20:8. *Remember the sabbath day, to keep it holy.*

Exodus 16:23-30. And he said unto them, This is that which the LORD hath said, To morrow is the rest of the holy sabbath unto the LORD: *bake that which ye will bake to day, and seethe that ye will seethe*; and that which remaineth over lay up for you to be kept until the morning. And they laid it up till the morning, as Moses bade: and it did not stink, neither was there any worm therein. And Moses said, *Eat that to day; for to day is a sabbath unto the LORD: to day ye shall not find it in the field.* Six days ye shall gather it; but on the seventh day, which is the sabbath, in it there shall be none. And it came to pass, that there went out some of the people on the seventh day for to gather, and they found none. And the LORD said unto Moses, How long refuse ye to keep my commandments and my laws? See, for that the LORD hath given you the sabbath, therefore he giveth you on the sixth day the bread of two days; abide ye every man in his place, *let no man go out of his place on the seventh day.* So the people rested on the seventh day.

Exodus 31:15-17. Six days may work be done; but in the seventh is the sabbath of rest, holy to the LORD: *whosoever doeth any work in the sabbath day, he shall surely be put to death.* Wherefore the children of Israel shall *keep the sabbath, to observe the sabbath* throughout their generations, for a perpetual covenant. It is a sign between me and the children of Israel for ever: for in six days the LORD made heaven and earth, and *on the seventh day he rested, and was refreshed.*

Isaiah 58:13. *If thou turn away thy foot from the sabbath, from doing thy pleasure on my holy day*; and call the sabbath a delight, the holy of the LORD, honourable; and shalt honour him, *not doing thine own ways, nor finding thine own pleasure, nor speaking thine own words.*

Nehemiah 13:15-19, 21-22. In those days saw I in Judah some treading wine presses on the sabbath, and bringing in sheaves, and lading asses; as also wine, grapes, and figs, and all manner of burdens, which they brought into Jerusalem on the sabbath day: and I testified against them in the day wherein they sold victuals. There dwelt men of Tyre also therein, which brought fish, and all manner of ware, and sold on the sabbath unto the children of Judah, and in Jerusalem. Then I contended with the nobles of Judah, and said unto them, What evil thing is this that ye do, and profane the sabbath day? Did not your fathers thus, and did not our God bring all this evil upon us, and upon this city? yet ye bring more wrath upon Israel by profaning the sabbath. And it came to pass, that when the gates of Jerusalem began to be dark before the sabbath, I commanded that the gates should be shut, and charged that they should not be opened till after the sabbath: and some of my servants set I at the gates, that

also are taken up the whole time in the public and private exercises of his worship, and in the duties of necessity and mercy.[145]

---

there should no burden be brought in on the sabbath day. Then I testified against them, and said unto them, Why lodge ye about the wall? if ye do so again, I will lay hands on you. From that time forth came they no more on the sabbath. And I commanded the Levites that they should cleanse themselves, and that they should come and keep the gates, to sanctify the sabbath day. Remember me, O my God, concerning this also, and spare me according to the greatness of thy mercy.

145 Isaiah 58:13. *If thou turn away thy foot from the sabbath, from doing thy pleasure on my holy day*; and call the sabbath a delight, the holy of the LORD, honourable; and shalt honour him, *not doing thine own ways, nor finding thine own pleasure, nor speaking thine own words.*
Matthew 12:1-13. At that time Jesus went on the sabbath day through the corn; and his disciples were an hungered, and began to pluck the ears of corn, and to eat. But when the Pharisees saw it, they said unto him, Behold, thy disciples do that which is not lawful to do upon the sabbath day. But he said unto them, Have ye not read what David did, when he was an hungered, and they that were with him; how he entered into the house of God, and did eat the shewbread, which was not lawful for him to eat, neither for them which were with him, but only for the priests? Or have ye not read in the law, how that on the sabbath days the priests in the temple profane the sabbath, and are blameless? But I say unto you, That in this place is one greater than the temple. But if ye had known what this meaneth, I will have mercy, and not sacrifice, ye would not have condemned the guiltless. For the Son of man is Lord even of the sabbath day. And when he was departed thence, he went into their synagogue: and, behold, there was a man which had his hand withered. And they asked him, saying, Is it lawful to heal on the sabbath days? that they might accuse him. And he said unto them, What man shall there be among you, that shall have one sheep, and if it fall into a pit on the sabbath day, will he not lay hold on it, and lift it out? How much then is a man better than a sheep? Wherefore it is lawful to do well on the sabbath days. Then saith he to the man, Stretch forth thine hand. And he stretched it forth; and it was restored whole, like as the other.